MIRACLES THROUGH HELL

A TRUE STORY OF HOLOCAUST SURVIVAL AND INTERGENERATIONAL HEALING

JERRY M. ELMAN

WATERVIEW BOOKS

CONTENTS

APPENDIXES

Cover Design by Autumn Raven
Edited by Jessie Atkin, Yasmin Gruss and Christine LePorte
Book layout by Autumn Raven
Photography by Jerry Elman

Waterview Books Honeoye, NY

In honor of the partisans who fled and fought, those who hid in the forests, those who survived the death camps, and those who survived the pogroms after liberation.
In memory of the six million Jews who perished. They shall remain in our hearts and souls forever.
In memory of my parents, Shmeryl and Rochal Elman.
In memory of all my family members who survived and have since passed away.
In memory of all my family members who perished in the Holocaust. You will never be forgotten.
In memory of the heroic Christians who risked the lives of their families to save Jews from certain death.

"*Throughout history, it has been the inaction of those who could have acted, the indifference of those who should have known better, the silence of the voice of justice when it mattered most, that has made it possible for evil to triumph.*"

— HAILE SELASSIE

ACKNOWLEDGMENTS

My thanks and love to my wife, Janet, son, David, and daughter, Sandi, for their strength, understanding, and support through all the years it took me to figure myself out.

My gratitude and love to the Hav for thirty-six-plus years of genuine friendship and your encouragement to write this book. Genuine friends are hard to find—they are precious when you do!

My best wishes to my brother, Benjamin, who was nine months old when he and our parents left the destruction of Europe and came to America. His early years were spent in a tough neighborhood while our parents struggled to build a new life. He persevered and became a world-acclaimed academic. Today, he battles Parkinson's disease. My thoughts and prayers will always be with him.

PREFACE

On November 1, 1942, my mother, Rochal Gritczak, was fourteen years old, living with her family in Sokoly, a small village in Poland. The Germans had just announced the liquidation (the large-scale transport of Jews to death camps) of the Jews of Sokoly. Her father planned the family's escape as the liquidation of the ghetto began. They had no idea of the absolute hell they would face. The betrayals. The miracles that would keep them alive. And they learned that even when surrounded by masses who embraced evil, the good of just a few is enough to make the difference for many.

On the night of January 31, 1943, a group of young people escaped from the ghetto in Pruzhany, Poland. Two people in this group were my father, Shmeryl Elman, age twenty-two, and my uncle, Yossel Elman, nineteen. Temperatures were below zero. Dressed in white linen to camouflage their appearance against the snow on the ground, they made a run for the ghetto fence in complete darkness. They quickly slid under the cut wires and ran for freedom to nearby forests.

There were fifteen men and three women in this group. They had made plans, dug bunkers within the ghetto, and stored a cache of supplies and weapons. A partially completed tunnel was not ready for the escape. Time had not allowed for the tunnel's completion or finishing other preparations. The liquidation of the Pruzhany ghetto was underway. It would take four days to liquidate the ghetto of ten thousand Jews. It was now or never to escape for this group approaching the fence. German guards shot at them as they breached the ghetto fence. They had already decided they would get through or die trying.

None of these people had a clue of what miracles and hell they would face after this attempt to escape. All they knew was that if they were to die, it would be on their terms, not Hitler's. They sought revenge, not survival. They had no idea of the collective impact of their efforts. They changed the course of a war, the course of history. One by one, they showed the world that the human spirit is a powerful force, no matter the odds.

I have captured the true stories of my parents' Holocaust survival as accurately as possible. Without hearing each individual account, one cannot understand the miracles and hell of hiding or being a partisan (a member of an armed resistance group fighting the Germans in World War II). Every survivor's story has two key themes: the absolute hell they faced and the countless miracles that kept them alive.

The children of Holocaust survivors are known as "second generation survivors." Most survivors lived by a "code of silence." This silence was meant to shield their children from the horrors of their survival, but it did the opposite. Their silence kept us always wondering about their past. The family members lost—our roots. We could see their emotional pain as much as they tried to hide it. We could not understand it. We suffered from our own scars, even nightmares. We did not understand why. We would always hear the slogan "Never forget" when the Holocaust was mentioned in the synagogue or public remembrance. But we always asked ourselves, "Never forget what?"

In the 1970s, the emotional and psychological struggles of children of Holocaust survivors had been formally discovered. While not born during the Holocaust, the second generation inherited a legacy of trauma through the behavioral patterns of their parents and their parents' silence about their trauma.

My father passed away in 1989, my mother in 2004. All my survivor grandparents, aunts, uncles, and cousins have passed away—all with their stories untold. If I did not tell their stories, they would be lost forever. And I would never free myself from always wondering. And even worse, my children and their children would never know our family history and their connection to the Holocaust.

Most survivors are no longer alive today. Holocaust denial is becoming mainstream. Fascism, even in America, is on the rise. For these reasons, these stories of survival must be understood and preserved.

Writing this book has been a personal journey for me, in ways I never imagined. Because the silent survivors of the Holocaust unknowingly passed on emotional scars to their children, those of us in the next generation have scars and demons in our heads that we have never understood, nightmares when we sleep that we cannot explain. This personal journey has helped me understand my trauma and my battle with depression. Through the telling of my family history, my story is also told.

THEN AND NOW

My parents survived the Holocaust, as did my uncle and other members of my family. Most of my family did not survive. I am a first-generation American, part of the next generation of survivors.

My parents did not meet until after their liberation by the Russians. Their stories are both the same and different—the same as far as the horrors and atrocities they lived through; different as far as where they lived and how they survived.

I grew up like most in the next generation. Our parents kept their dark past to themselves. Their lives and experiences were never shared with or understood by their families. We grew up with no roots or history aside from knowing they survived the Holocaust. .

I have lived with questions that were never answered. What are my roots? Who were the family members who perished whom I never knew? What was life in Europe like before the Holocaust? How did my parents and other relatives survive, and what did that even mean? What did they experience and endure to survive? What was their impact on the course of the war? So many questions I never dared ask my parents when they were alive. Questions they would not have answered if I did.

They wanted their children to believe their lives started with a clean slate after their arrival in America. The Holocaust was a historical event they would occasionally mention, something we would read about in history books. It never became personal. Beyond that, it was like reading about the Civil War and other wars. It happened.

When I was growing up, other families and friends shared their histories, roots, and traditions. When I was asked, my answer was always straight and quick: "My parents are Holocaust survivors from Europe. Most of my family perished. I don't know much else." (These three sentences would have made up the entire contents of this book if not for the research I conducted!) After I gave that answer, people would quickly change the subject.

To be honest, I did know a few stories, but just in bits and pieces. My father would talk to me about life lessons he learned from the Holocaust and sometimes about life as a partisan. My mother would never talk about it at all, and if she did, she would share her bitterness, not the details of what she lived through.

Most second generation survivors learned to stop asking questions. We understood our parents did not want to talk about it. They gave different signals when we brought it up. When we were young, the answer was always, "You are too young. We can talk when you are older." When we were older, asking would create a sudden change in their mood. The looks on their faces became solemn, sad, or annoyed. They would respond, "You don't need to know." They would change the subject. Sometimes, they would be as honest as possible and say it was too difficult to talk about.

We buried our curiosity and our desire to know. Before we knew it, we were out of the house—adults and raising our own families. And then, our parents passed away. But the need to know was always there. There would be no closure in our lives as the next generation if we did not know their stories. I did not want to let my life go by without filling in the blanks of my family history.

I retired in 2021. Current events brought a greater sense of urgency to get the answers I sought. I witnessed the turmoil of the 2016 and 2020 presidential elections. The COVID pandemic continues to disrupt the entire world. The insurrection at the US Capitol. The "Big Lie" about the 2020 election threatening American democracy. Voting laws to restrict voting. Seeing millions of people refuse to do something as simple as wearing a mask to protect others or take a vaccine that could save their lives. Unarmed Black people keep getting killed by police for no reason other than being Black. Today, Americans live in a time when an entire political party is focused on power, control, fascism, and dictatorship.

The daily news highlights this growing hatred and fascism in a nation once known as the beacon of democracy and freedom. Our institutions are being attacked and delegitimized. The rise of antisemitism, racism, hate of immigrants, and hate for women and women's rights are becoming new norms.

America is so divided that I do not know it anymore.

I felt worried and scared about the future as a Jew and an American. I started asking myself, "Is this what my parents experienced with the rise of Hitler and the Nazi Party? Is history going to repeat itself? But what history?" I did not know what my parents and the other survivors lived through.

But I did know that it only took one political party preaching hatred and fascism to bring Hitler to power. Hitler failed with his first coup. He succeeded with his second. America has already had one attempted coup. Would there be another? People were forming militias and preparing for another coup. I was now scared. I told myself, "This must be how my parents felt. I must get the answers and stories now because it is no longer just the past. It could be the future if we don't understand and stop it!"

So, I began the research. I started with a thick folder of documents my father had left. There was a box of pictures. I also found the Yizkor (memorial) books written in Yiddish for Jewish communities across Europe. I found a translator for all the Yiddish material. I searched the online archives of worldwide organizations that kept records of the Holocaust. I reached out to other family members, most of whom are in Israel. I read numerous books, several of which contained specific information about my parents. Through all these sources, I uncovered more details than I ever expected. I corroborated most of the information to make the stories as accurate as possible.

I have learned that all stories about Holocaust survivors include betrayal, bravery, determination, luck, and fate. Each has situation after situation where death is beaten, not once, but hundreds of times. Each of them met miracle after miracle that saved their lives.

Holocaust survivors had a significant impact on the outcome of the war. They were not just "survivors." My father and uncle were two Jewish partisans who fought shoulder to shoulder with tens of thousands of others to defeat the Germans in World War II. They saved the lives of thousands of Jews, Christians, and allied troops. The partisans blew up bridges and railroads, cut down telephone poles, and destroyed military transports. They wiped out German garrisons and killed German officers, all with unyielding willpower against all odds.

Most people, including myself, viewed the partisans as unorganized ragtag groups who hid in the forests and attacked the Germans. They started in that perceived image, but they grew into highly organized, well-trained, well-supplied fierce fighting groups.

The Russian-led partisan groups in Belarus were a significant factor in the defeat of the German army. Overall, they disrupted 30 to 40 percent of the German supply chain to the Russian front. The Germans also had to divert three divisions from the Russian front back to Belarus to fight the partisans and repair all the blown up transportation and communication systems. And once repaired, they got blown up again!

In 1944, there were 374,000 Belarusian partisans in total. About 25,000 were Jews like my father and uncle. From June 1941 to July 1944, Belarusian partisans killed about 500,000 members of the German military and their local collaborators. They undermined and derailed around 11,000 regular German trains and more than thirty armored trains. They destroyed around thirty railway stations and almost 1,000 headquarters and garrisons. They blasted, burned, and destroyed more than 800 railroad bridges and nearly 5,000 other bridges. They destroyed more than 7,300 kilometers of telephone and telegraph lines. They shot down more than 300 airplanes and destroyed more than 1,300 tanks and armored vehicles and almost 1,000 weapons depots.

One highlight of the Belarusian partisan war against the Germans was the September 22, 1943, assassination of Wilhelm Kube, the leader of the occupation administration of Belarus. A woman partisan became a worker in his house and placed a bomb under his bed. She escaped and survived.

My mother, Rochal (Gritczak) Elman, went into hiding with her parents and sisters. Through determination, luck, and fate, they survived against all odds. Her father's long-term relationships with Christians made the difference for them. An honest and honorable man, he was a well-known leather and fur trader among Jews and Christians. He bought leather and furs from many Christian farmers in Sokoly and around the nearby city of Bialystok. It was not just business to Zeev, as he also developed many friendships with the Christian farmers. He would help them with interest-free loans when they needed money. He would bring food for their families, hay for their farms, and provide other supplies if they could not afford to purchase them. He helped the people he knew in any way he could. He rarely asked others for anything other than their loyal business and friendship. He was one of the few Jews well-known and respected by Christian farmers. Several of these farmers helped save the lives of Zeev and his family during the Holocaust. They did this at significant risk to themselves and their families. These farmers were part of a minority of Christians across Poland who did the right thing and saved Jews.

My mother and her sisters were very young and lost their adolescent years to the war. My mother was fourteen when it started. When the war ended, she was seventeen, married to my father, and a mother at eighteen.

My research found less information about my mother and her family before the war than I could find about my father and his family. There was minimal information about my grandmother and her side of the family. I hope to fill this gap over time.

Each story talks about the suffering and conditions of pure hell survivors endured. Most survivors downplayed their bravery by saying their survival was due to luck, knowledge, and opportunity. I have concluded that they were courageous heroes. Their luck, knowledge, and opportunity are better defined as the miracles that saved them. Their stories of survival demonstrated that the human spirit can prevail under the most horrible conditions.

LIFE IN PRUZHANY BEFORE 1939

M y father, Shmeryl Elman, and his brother, Yossel's, story starts in Pruzhany, Poland (now Belarus).

Pruzhany always had a large and active Jewish community. Jews made up about 57 percent of the population and played an active role in the community's political life. Jews could participate in the municipal government when Poland became independent in 1919. In 1927, sixteen of the twenty-four delegates elected to the municipal administration were Jews.

Shmeryl and Yossel Elman's father, Binyamin, moved to Pruzhany to attend a yeshiva (an Orthodox Jewish seminary) as a teenager. He later became a teacher and met his future wife, Seryl Kaplan, whose father, Chaim Kaplan, was a wealthy farmer and owned a large flour mill. Seryl's mother's family also owned a brewery, a one-hundred-acre dairy farm, and a soybean oil mill.

Binyamin and Seryl married and had four children. Shmeryl was the oldest, born in 1919. Yossel was next, then came a daughter, Chaika, and then another daughter, Shayndl. They were all three years apart in age.

The children were closest to their mother's family because

they lived in Pruzhany. Only Binyamin's father and half sister, Chaska, who lived in the town of Chomsk, remained in Poland.

Binyamin's other siblings—one brother and four sisters—had immigrated to the United States. Binyamin's father was married three times, and each wife was younger than the last. His siblings in America were much older than him; Binyamin's father's first wife was their mother. His second wife was Chaska's mother, and his third wife was Binyamin's mother.

Binyamin's brother, Samuel Elman, was the oldest and immigrated to the United States in 1891. Samuel then made it possible for his four sisters to join him in America. Binyamin was much younger than his siblings, newly married, and starting a family. Seryl's entire family was in Pruzhany, so Binyamin declined his brother Samuel's offer to join the rest of the Elmans in the United States. Binyamin stayed in touch with his siblings in America. Samuel sent money to help the family out a few times a year.

Binyamin and Seryl bought a house in the middle of town. He obtained a tobacco concession license and opened a tobacco factory and small tobacco store in the market square. Binyamin was active in shul (synagogue), serving as a Torah reader and occasionally as the cantor (leading the congregation in song and music during prayer). The family was religious. All Jews observed Shabbat, and shops shut down mid-afternoon on Fridays with its impending arrival. Seryl's father, Abraham Kaplan, would conduct kiddush (the blessing over wine and bread) after Shabbat services and before the family meal.

The family spoke Yiddish at home and within the Jewish community. Yiddish was the universal language spoken by all European Jews. They spoke Polish in public school and among Christians.

Pruzhany had a thriving Jewish community, including merchants, tradespeople, and scholars. There was a sizable Jewish market area in Pruzhany with about one hundred shops.

The family lived a modest life and tried to be as self-sufficient as possible. On their property was a large vegetable garden.

Chickens, ducks, and geese lived on a small pond. On their large side porch, Seryl planted pots of geraniums. The house was large and roomy. Seryl loved to bake bread in the large brick oven in the kitchen. The pond on their property would freeze over in the winter, and the Elman children would ice skate with their friends.

Shmeryl attended a Hebrew high school that required his father to pay tuition. His father struggled with the tobacco business, so it was challenging to finance Shmeryl's education. At first, having a tobacco license meant exclusive rights to manufacture and sell tobacco in the town. Then, the Polish government opened tobacco manufacturing and sales to others to take business away from the exclusive Jewish tobacco merchants. Later, the Polish government nationalized the tobacco business and seized Binyamin's tobacco factory and store. Jews could no longer be in this business. He received compensation, but nowhere near what the business and property were worth. Seryl's father owned two grain mills, so Binyamin joined his father-in-law's business selling grain.

With the financial hardship of losing his tobacco business, Binyamin could no longer afford the school tuition, so Shmeryl dropped out after eighth grade. He did not want to attend a Polish public school. He then helped his father and worked other odd jobs to earn some money for the family. Yossel attended a public school and continued his high school education until the German occupation in 1941. It was a challenging time for Binyamin. He was a proud man, and the struggle to support his family impacted his self-esteem. While his in-laws were wealthy, he would not take anything from them other than a job selling grain.

Shmeryl and Yossel became active in the Zionist youth group. (Zionism was a worldwide movement that believed in establishing a Jewish nation in what later became Israel.) The Zionist movement became popular with the youth across all Jewish communities in Poland. This belief was driven by worldwide antisemitism, and the life of fear Jews lived as minorities in other countries. Specific to Poland, the Jewish youth were fed up with the long-standing mistreatment of Jews and believed antisemitism would always be prevalent there. They wanted to leave Poland for a Jewish state in British mandate Palestine.

The adults and senior generations viewed things differently. They aligned with the Yiddishe politics, which promoted keeping their lives and traditions in Poland like the generations before them. They believed that Jews would be equal to Polish Christians in the future. They refused to believe there was any threat from Germany with the rise of Hitler and the Nazis. As far as they were concerned, all of that was happening in Germany, not Poland. It did not affect them. But the youth saw it differently. They saw Polish antisemitism worsening as Hitler's propaganda made it into Poland.

Shmeryl was a Zionist; however, he did not aspire to move to Palestine. He wanted to join the rest of the Elman family, his uncle, and his aunts in America. Shmeryl viewed the conflict between the Arabs and Jews in Palestine and the British support of attacks against Jews as bad or worse than Poland. He viewed America as a safe haven for Jews based on the success and happiness of his family there. In 1936, Shmeryl applied for an American visa. The Polish quota for American visas was small and backed up for years, so he had to wait.

The following was written in Yiddish by Shmeryl Elman in 1975 about his early upbringing:

I was born in 1919 in Pruzhany, a God-forsaken shtetl in Poland, between Kobryn and Brest, eighteen km off Warsaw-Moscow Road. My father was a teacher in Pruzhany. Later he tried his hand at different commercial enterprises. One was a small cigarette factory until the monopoly on tobacco was established, then a tobacco shop, followed by grain trade. He didn't make any money out of these businesses and was barely able to provide for his family with four children, two sons and two daughters. My mother was one of two daughters of a landowner of Shimentsy farm, owned jointly with a son and a son-in-law.

I received my first education in cheders (Jewish/Hebrew elementary schools), the first one with the Szereszów [now Sharashova, Belarus] rabbi, the second with the Kossow [now Kosava, Belarus] rabbi. This was followed by four years of classes in Yavneh Hebrew school, and then one more year in Tarbut secondary school. I only completed the eighth grade as my father was no longer able to pay for my education despite the fact that I was a good student and wanted to continue with my studies. Unfortunately, my grandfather wasn't willing to help out with my further schooling. In his opinion, it wasn't important enough.

With the outbreak of WWII and as a consequence of the Final Solution of the Jewish question in Poland by the Germans, all property, big or small, fell into the hands of non-Jewish strangers.

From what I can remember of my youth, even though in those days Jewish education was leaning toward passivity toward Polish antisemitism and not altering the way of life which had continued for hundreds, and even thousands, of years, I had the inclination toward defiance, toward not letting others influence me, and toward opposing certain circumstances. To this day, I'm not sure from whom I inherited this inclination. But the fact is that later in life, this inclination proved to be very helpful in making firm decisions and adapting to various circumstances. All this taken together molded my character, will and outlook that later broke every barrier of courage and endurance, enabling me to keep going against the coming storm.

The Elman family, 1936 (left to right, Yossel, Seryl,
Shmeryl, Binyamin, Chaika. Center, Shayndl)

Left to right Shayndl and Chaika Elman, 1939

Shmeryl Elman, 1937

3

LIFE IN SOKOLY BEFORE 1939

My mother, Rochal Gritczak, and her family lived in a small town named Sokoly.

Sokoly had about 2,500 residents. It was near the city of Bialystok. I do not know how or when her father, Zeev, and her mother, Menucha, met. Zeev and Menucha's parents also lived in Sokoly. Sheinche was the oldest daughter, then Rochal, then a son, Yudel, and then another daughter, Mina.

Sokoly was a respected center of Jewish art, scholarship, and culture for two hundred years. Highly educated doctors, rabbis, scholars, and artists lived there. As a result, Sokoly's Jewish cultural, religious, and social life thrived. There were several synagogues, charitable and public institutions, and Jewish schools.

The primary source of income for Jews came from being craft workers, small merchants, and peddlers. Everyone struggled. Poverty was prevalent. Many Jewish merchants and peddlers had business relationships with Polish farmers outside Sokoly. These farmers were not antisemitic, and they treated Jews well. During the German occupation, many of these farmers aided and hid Jews.

Life for the Jews in Sokoly before World War II was

dangerous. Most of the Jewish population lived in separate Jewish settlements in the area. Jews who had previously lived among the Christian population in the town had to flee the intense antisemitic pressure of their non-Jewish neighbors. Robberies, arson, and murder were common for Jews if they ventured out of their settlements or into town.

Antisemitism was at the center of sermons every Sunday in the Catholic churches. The Jews were the killers of Christ. They drank the blood of Christian children. They were communists. They controlled all the money, and on and on. The Polish Catholic Church institutionalized the hate of Jews. This legitimized violence toward Jews.

The Poles regularly threw stones at Jewish people walking on the streets. Next to the Jewish shops, gangs of young Polish ruffians (or "pikatniks") would hang out with clubs and sticks in their hands. They would beat Jews, and they also would block Christians from entering Jewish stores to shop. Occasionally, the pikatniks would break windows in Jewish houses and shops during the market and fair days. Jewish kiosks and shops were destroyed. They stole merchandise and took the kerosene that Jews would carry home for fuel and lanterns. They attacked and beat Jews leaving the yeshiva, often killing them. They attacked and killed Jewish merchants and peddlers doing business with nearby farmers outside of the village.

There was no police enforcement protecting Jews and no punishment for stealing, hurting, or killing Jews.

Jews accepted this way of life for generations. It became the norm to live and survive among a majority of antisemites. To be fair, there were many Polish Catholics who were not antisemitic and treated Jews well. Most of them were rural farmers who conducted business and traded with Jews. Zeev Gritczak and his father had close relationships with many Polish Christian farmers. During the Holocaust, many of these Polish farmers were heroes. They hid Jews at risk of death for their entire family if caught.

So, under this history and backdrop, the Gritczak family lived in Sokoly. In a large house, the family lived with Zeev's parents,

Yaacov and Sarah Gritczak. Zeev had a brother who immigrated to America many years earlier. Zeev worked with his father, Yaacov, in the leather and fur trading business. They were successful.

Menucha grew up in a summer resort town ten kilometers from Sokoly. She had six sisters who grew up in a mansion owned by her parents. One of her sisters took over the home with her family after their parents had passed away. The Gritczak family would spend time each summer staying at the mansion. For the children, it was like going to summer camp.

The Gritczak family was small, only Zeev and his parents, as his brother had left for America years before. Zeev was close to his parents. They had a large house, which allowed his family to live with them.

There were only Polish public schools in Sokoly. No Jewish or Hebrew schools existed. Sheinche attended Hebrew school in the nearby city of Bialystok, staying with her father's friends. The Zionist youth movement thrived in Sokoly. Most Jewish youths participated in the movement's activities, aspiring to future lives in Palestine.

On September 1, 1939, the German army invaded Poland. At once, the Polish military collapsed. Polish soldiers attacked and ransacked Jewish homes in retreat.

The Germans burned the entire Jewish area of the nearby district city, Wysokie Mazowieckie. They forced the Jews into the synagogue there and burned it down with them packed inside. They shot or beat the rest to death. Not a single Jew remained alive that did not escape. Many fled to Sokoly.

The next day German soldiers entered Sokoly. They came through on motorcycles first. After that, the tanks came through. Then, the troops on foot.

They began a rampage against Jews. Guided by the antisemitic Poles who identified Jewish addresses, they ransacked homes and abducted Jewish community leaders.

They captured the rabbi, Yossef Rosenblum, and tortured him for days. They stripped him of his clothing, and when he was barefoot and almost naked, they forced him to jump and dance in the streets while many Germans and Poles used sticks and whips to strike his exposed back. They also captured large numbers of observant Jewish men with beards. They beat these men and ripped their beards off with the flesh.

The Germans pushed a frightened crowd of Jews into the old synagogue, threatening to burn it down with them inside. They kept these captives terrified for many hours and then released them.

While the homes were in flames, the Germans and Poles rushed around the town's streets like hunting dogs and captured Jews with the possessions they had rescued from their burning homes. Later, they gathered hundreds of Jews and forced them into the Catholic church.

The Germans threatened to take revenge on the prisoners because Poles killed three of their soldiers in the village of Lachy (three kilometers from Sokoly). The Germans burned Lachy and murdered a few farmers in retaliation. But without the addition of Jewish victims, they did not regard their revenge as complete.

Five hundred imprisoned Jews in Sokoly lay in fear of death all night.

The church's doors opened at seven o'clock in the morning, and a few Germans entered. They ordered the prisoners to get up and form lines according to age; thirty and up, twenty to twenty-nine, and youngsters up to the age of nineteen.

At first, they thought the Germans were going to shoot them according to the order of the lines. Broken-hearted parents separated from their children, and siblings were torn from other siblings. Unexpectedly, while in line, the Jews were told they could leave. The German's sole purpose was to instill terror and fear.

The day after this night of horrors, a series of searches began. Germans and Poles commandeered wealthy Jewish houses. They walked house to house, searching for gold, jewelry, leather, manufactured merchandise, bed linen, and other expensive possessions, which the Jews hid. They uncovered hidden cellars, false walls, and double attics that held fine china, silver, linen, jewelry, and other goods. All of it was seized.

The Gritczak family remained in their house all this time, too scared to come out. They had run out of food. A Christian friend stopped over to check on them. He brought a sack of prunes, supplying them with something to eat. Later, German soldiers came to the house to search for items they could seize. They found nothing. They then asked what was in the sack. When they were told it contained prunes, they ripped the sack apart and threw the prunes all over the house.

The Poles showed the Germans where attractive Jewish girls lived. In the evenings, they then went to those houses and raped them. A bitter panic arose as word of this got out. Many young girls of Sokoly hid in barns, attics, and cellars. Some escaped from the village to the homes of Christian farmers they knew who protected them.

During this time, Jews did not lie down to sleep. They all lived in fear. The Germans continued to kidnap Jews they could brutalize.

The horror continued for twelve days. Suddenly, the Germans left, and then the Russians came in. Sokoly was in the part of Poland that Russia would now control. The situation in town reversed. The Jews were ecstatic, while the Poles were unhappy and afraid of the Russians.

The Russians searched for Poles who collaborated with the Germans and Jews, whom they viewed as agitators and a threat to communist control. They sent these people to Russia. After the Russian army arrived, a new civil administration took over. They accepted both Jews and Poles in all institutions without discrimination. They implemented the communist system. All property and businesses became nationalized under communism. People had to rent their homes from the government. They had to buy their goods from government-owned shops. No one owned anything. Everyone received pay for their work from the government. Because the communist system created a shortage of all food and goods, an underground economy developed where people traded among themselves for goods and services.

While the Jews did not like the communist system, they felt safe under Russian control. The Poles could not harass the Jews. The Jews returned to a stable life.

Left to right, Menucha and Zeev Gritczak, year unknown

Left to right, Rochal and Yudel Gritczak, date unknown

Left to right, Rochal, Sheinche, Mina, and Yudel Gritczak
before the war

4

PRUZHANY OCCUPATION

W hen the German army invaded Poland and approached Pruzhany, the Polish military quickly retreated, attacking Jewish neighborhoods in all the places they passed through. They looted Jewish homes, beating up and even killing Jews. Many Poles welcomed the Germans. They viewed Russia as a more significant threat and thought the Germans would protect them. Plus, they shared a common hatred of Jews with the Germans.

Pruzhany Jews feared that the peasants and Christians who lived nearby would also attack. Before war broke out, regular pogroms (organized massacres of Jewish people in Eastern Europe and Russia) took place. The disarray made it easy to attack, loot, and even kill Jews. So, Shmeryl, Yossel, and others organized a large group of men to patrol and protect the Jewish area of Pruzhany. They also dug ditches in the dirt roads to make things more difficult for potential attackers. They had no weapons but believed being visible in large numbers would be enough of a deterrent. Fortunately, they were right. There was no attack or pogrom.

Within days, German advance units came through Pruzhany

but continued west and did not stop. The Germans were not formally occupying Pruzhany and the surrounding area. This confused people. They did not know that Hitler and Stalin had signed a peace agreement that split Poland between Germany and Russia. Russia would annex the parts of Belarus and Ukraine under Polish rule, and the rest of Poland would fall to German occupation. They had agreed that German forces would attack Poland first. Then, as soon as the German army reached the River Boog, Russian troops would cross the border and attack Poland from the east. The Russian military arrived in Pruzhany on September 18, 1939.

The Russians created immediate shortages of goods and merchandise. Soldiers of the Russian army saw all the businesses full of goods they had never seen in their hometowns. They carried Russian rubles and bought everything in the stores in massive quantities. Suddenly, all stores were empty, and merchants had nothing more to sell. Everyone knew the communist system would keep store shelves bare. The people of Pruzhany would now have to live life like Russians—in long lines, with nothing available to buy.

Shmeryl Elman could not tolerate life under Russian rule. Later in 1939, he tried to escape by making his way to Vilna. Once there, Shmeryl would go to the American Consulate and attempt to get a visa to America. His application submitted in 1936 was still in the system. He thought his new situation might give him an excellent case for political asylum, but he could not get to Vilna. Thousands of people filled the train stations. Refugees were all trying to do the same thing.

Since it was impossible to get to Vilna, Shmeryl traveled to the Romanian border to get to the American Consulate there, but he faced the same situation. In talking with other refugees, he got scolded for what he was trying to do. They were trying to flee German-controlled areas. He was trying to escape Russian control. They told him he should appreciate being under Russian control instead of living under Nazi rule. Living a communist life was far better than certain death under the Nazis. They said they would trade places with him anytime! Shmeryl, seeing that his effort was futile, returned to Pruzhany.

The Russians implemented the communist system quickly. All private business and property now belonged to the state. The Russian government controlled all commerce through cooperative factories and shops. They set up a cooperative in Pruzhany, but there were no goods to be found. When goods arrived, they were in small quantities, never enough to meet the demand. People would form long lines in the morning, not even knowing what would be available to buy that day. Their efforts were often in vain as the supply ran out quickly.

Over time, an underground economy came into place. People would barter and trade among themselves. Soon, there was an ample supply of goods through the underground effort.

Synagogues were closed and used as storage facilities. All Jewish institutions and schools were closed and seized. The Russians took control of everything under the Russian system.

The Russians began a campaign of arrests, executions, and expulsion to work camps in Siberia, targeting Polish figures of authority such as military officers, police, and priests. They also targeted Jews who were Zionist leaders, intellectuals whose philosophies conflicted with communism, and those who resisted Russian control.

On January 15, 1940, the town of Pruzhany became the center of the newly formed Pruzhany district, which was part of the Brest region of the Belarus Russian Socialist Republic.

Under Russian occupation, the Jews felt fortunate when they heard what was happening in German-occupied Poland and beyond. Mostly, the Russians left the Jews alone if they did not create problems or trouble.

In June 1941, there were rumors that Germany was planning a war with Russia. The Russian leaders in Pruzhany and elsewhere did not take these rumors seriously and dismissed them. People were continually told that the German-Russian alliance was rock solid. Even Joseph Stalin believed this. How wrong they turned out to be.

The morning of June 21, 1941, most people were awakened by heavy bombardment of the Pruzhany airport, which was built by the Russians and used as an air force base and munitions depot. The explosions were seen in the sky. No one knew what was going on. Some thought these were Russian military exercises.

It soon became clear the airplanes in the sky were German, not Russian. A crushing offensive by the German military on the unprepared Russians was underway. No Russian airplanes were able to take off. They were all destroyed on the ground.

Germany successfully launched a full-fledged war against Russia under total surprise. Two hundred Russian divisions, forming the first line of defense, retreated as fast as possible without a fight. The Germans promptly occupied Belarus and moved toward Moscow. Within days, the German army breached the entire Russian front.

After the German invasion, tens of thousands of retreating Russian commanders and troops were trapped behind German lines, unable to get back to their retreating Russian army units. Instead, they self-organized into Russian partisan units to fight the Germans in the forests. The Jews who later fled would not have survived had this not happened.

June 23, 1941, was a beautiful summer day in Pruzhany. The streets were empty. The entire village waited in fear for the pending arrival of German troops. They arrived at midday. No Jews appeared outside. They remained in their homes, afraid of what was about to happen to them. Christian residents were in the streets, celebrating the arrival of the Germans. They handed out flowers to the marching soldiers and gave them a joyous welcome. To the Poles, the Germans were their allies and the Russians the enemy. The Germans had liberated them from the Russians. The Poles shared their hatred of Jews.

The Christians helped the Germans identify and harass the Pruzhany Jews. Immediately, pillage began. Day and night, Germans and Poles plundered and beat Jews. They pulled the beards off observant Jewish men, flesh and all. Nights were terrible. Screams for aid came from assaulted houses. Jewish life became upended, and their possessions were looted.

For three weeks, the wave of German army troops' transports, tanks, heavy equipment, ammunition, and supplies continued through Pruzhany on the main road between Brest-Litovsk and Moscow. The Germans sent three million soldiers to the Russian front. The German trucks and tanks that came through the first few days had banners on them: "14 days to Moscow!"

The day after the German administration took control, the Germans posted that all young men must report to the Pruzhany airport the following day. Shmeryl, now age twenty-one, and Yossel, age eighteen, had to take part.

When the Russians had retreated, they left thousands of barrels of airplane fuel at the airport, as well as airplane parts and large numbers of crates filled with weapons and munitions. The Germans assigned the Jews to various work details. Shmeryl ended up with a group that rolled all the barrels of airplane fuel to a central location at the airport. The German guards kept yelling at the men and whipped anyone they thought was not working fast enough. Shmeryl worked alongside a Russian who was captured in Pruzhany. The Russian started speaking to Shmeryl and told him the barrels were filled with schnapps (whiskey). A guard overheard them talking and walked over to them, demanding to know the nature of their conversation.

Shmeryl told the guard that the Russian said the barrels held schnapps. (Back in those days, airplane fuel was alcohol-based, and Russian soldiers drank it.) The German laughed, told them to stay where they were, and walked away into the nearby building. He came out holding a drinking glass. When he walked back to them, he handed the glass to the Russian and told him he had to drink a glass of airplane fuel.

With Shmeryl's help, the Russian removed a plug from the side of the barrel and allowed fuel to pour into the glass. They then plugged the barrel. The Russian, without hesitation, took the glass and drank it all down. The three of them then stood there for some time.

The German guard was expecting the Russian to get sick or die. The Russian remained standing; he was fine. The German then gave him a big pat on the back like a friend. He then looked at Shmeryl and said, "You don't seem to be afraid of me." Shmeryl responded, "No, why should I be? I am here to work." The German guard laughed and then told Shmeryl to stay where he was.

He then returned to the nearby building and came out with a can. He walked over to Shmeryl and told him to put the can on top of his head. Shmeryl nervously complied, knowing what was about to happen. The guard told him to stand in a nearby area, clear of other people and obstructions. The guard walked several yards away from Shmeryl and turned around, facing him. He then took his rifle and aimed it to shoot the can above Shmeryl's head. The guard fired, and Shmeryl fell backward.

Fortunately, the guard hit the can, but the impact of the shot at close range threw Shmeryl to the ground. His scalp got bruised, he had a terrible headache, and his vision became blurred. But there was no blood, and it became clear the bullet itself did not directly hit him.

The German guard laughed and ordered Shmeryl to get back to work. He had to work with that terrible headache and blurry vision for the rest of the day and then walk home. It took several days for Shmeryl to recover.

They assigned Yossel to a group that had to load airplane parts onto trucks. The German guard would yell at them and hit them with sticks and whips. Yossel and another person were told they had to load a crated airplane engine onto a truck. The engine weighed about one thousand pounds. Two people could not lift it. Guards beat them with sticks and whips as they tried to raise the crate. The Germans finally assigned a larger group of men to help. They could then put the engine in the truck.

Within a few weeks, the Gestapo entered Pruzhany to oversee the Jews. They asked the Christian leaders to provide eighteen names of Jews they strongly disliked. The Gestapo then gathered those eighteen people up one by one and arrested them. They took the group two kilometers out of town and ordered them to dig their graves. The Gestapo then shot all of them. The Gestapo was the most ruthless of Germans. There was absolutely no sense of humanity in their hearts. With joy, they killed, mutilated, and dismembered Jews.

The Germans created a civil police force made up of Poles. When it came to the Jews, the Germans knew the Poles would do all the dirty work for them.

For the Elman brothers, the German occupation gave them a keen sense of the dire future ahead of them.

The Gestapo command set up the Jewish ghetto (section of a city/town where Jews were forced to live) in July 1941. The Elman family could stay in their house, which was within the original boundary of the ghetto. In mid-1942, the Germans moved the boundaries to make the ghetto smaller. The Jews who lived outside the new boundary had to find other family members or friends to live with. The Elmans had to leave their house and move in with their grandparents.

With the Gestapo now in firm control, hunger became a problem for the Jews of Pruzhany. Christian peasants stopped selling their goods because they would not receive money as payment. They received other merchandise in exchange. This merchandise was worthless to them.

The Gestapo ordered the Jews to create a "Judenrat" (Jewish council) to manage the affairs of the Jewish community and meet all the demands made by the Gestapo. In the beginning, the Judenrat was small, composed of five members. Later, they ordered that it grow to twenty-four members. The larger Judenrat was required to handle all the administrative aspects of the ghetto along with the increasing German demands.

Every Jew now had to wear two yellow patches, one on the chest and one on the back. These yellow patches had a large Star of David with the word "Jude" in the middle. Every Jew, including small children, was now branded and visible to everyone.

The Gestapo forbade the Jews from walking on the sidewalks. Instead, they had to walk in the streets beside the drainage ditches.

The Germans and Poles beat, robbed, and even killed Jews out walking.

A group of Germans occupied a house behind the former Jewish seminary. Major Lehman led them. They were called "Lehman's Bandits." Their duties were to protect and maintain the telephone lines between the general German command and the front line. They were German military men. Their hate for Jews was one hundred times worse than that of the Gestapo or SS. Every few days, they would enter the ghetto, trap some Jews, and beat them fiercely. Or they would have their German shepherds attack them.

These murderers dragged the rabbi of Pruzhany, David Faigelboim, out of his house, dressed in his ritual tunic, tallit, and the tefillin. They pushed him through the streets during a heavy rainstorm to the quarters behind the town.

For forty-eight hours, they tortured him for no reason. The Jewish Judenrat paid a sizable ransom to free him from those criminal hands.

Shmeryl and Yossel Elman's uncle (their mother's sister's husband) owned a horse and wagon. The German Burger Meister (mayor) of Pruzhany regularly requested the Judenrat to provide Jews who owned horses and wagons, along with workers, to go out to the forest and cut down trees for firewood. They would load the wood into the wagons and come back to Pruzhany.

Lehman learned about this working group and decided he wanted a horse and wagon for his crew. One day, the workgroup left for the forest, and the Lehman Bandits attacked them with their dogs. Shmeryl and Yossel's uncle was torn apart and killed. It was a gruesome murder. Others received severe injuries. Shmeryl and Yossel's aunt was now a widow. One can only imagine the horror she felt when she learned the news of her husband's brutal murder.

5

THE GERMANS OCCUPY SOKOLY

On June 23, 1941, the German army was approaching Sokoly. The senior Russian officer, Major-General PP Kapusta, drove into town at noon. He was there to evacuate his staff from their headquarters in Sokoly. He would later become one of the most significant generals in command of the Russian partisans. Shmeryl Elman would later serve under General Kapusta in the partisans.

For seven days, the German army came through Sokoly but did not stop. Military vehicles, tanks, artillery, and more filled the major streets and continued without pause. They were rushing to begin the invasion of Russia after pushing the Russians out of Poland.

The Germans already occupied the nearby city of Bialystok. They captured 2,500 Jews with the help of Polish youths. They imprisoned the Jews inside the great synagogue and set it on fire. They also moved around the city, capturing other Jews throwing them into the burning synagogue's flames. They captured another 5,000 Jews and at once transported them to a death camp.

On the eighth day, a German commander and other officers arrived. The commander called for representatives of the Jews to come to him. The community selected a delegation led by Alter Ginzberg. The commander gave Alter Ginzberg the job of organizing the local Jewish council, the Judenrat, in Sokoly. As in other ghettos, the role of the Judenrat was to carry out German orders and demands and administer the Sokoly ghetto.

The commander demanded they create a list of all the merchandise the Jews owned. The German command seized all gold, silver, and jewelry. The commander warned them that searches would occur. Anyone found keeping gold, silver, valuable jewelry, and unlisted merchandise would face death.

The commander also ordered the Jews and Christians to hand over weapons, radio parts, and other objects left behind by the Soviets. Death would be the punishment for any delay in fulfilling these orders.

Sokoly was in a region of Poland that bordered Belarus. The Germans considered this area part of Poland and not Prussia, like Pruzhany. It was not part of the Third Reich. The Jews of Sokoly faced a much worse situation than the areas under direct German administration, like Pruzhany.

The Jews of Sokoly had to wear the yellow Star of David patch on the front and back of their clothing or coats, as was required in all other ghettos. Jews referred to it as the "badge of shame."

Patch kept by Rochal Gritczak that was never used.

The Germans beat Jews caught without the patches. They also had to pay a fine of ten marks. They gave the right to expel a Jew from their home to Germans, the Polish militia, the town administration, and any ordinary Christian. They seized all the expensive homes and possessions of wealthy Jews along with Jewish businesses. The Jews, now without homes, had to move in with relatives or other families.

Jews stayed inside their homes as much as possible. The threat of being caught by the Germans or Poles made the Jews terrified about what could happen to them if they were visible outside. Children would run away if they saw any Germans or Poles.

Sokoly was a small town compared to Pruzhany. A fence was not built around the ghetto area set up for Jews. Jews had to live in the ghetto, but they still could go anywhere in town. The Germans stationed guards at the town's perimeter, not the ghetto perimeter. It was easier for Jews to move around and even sneak out of the town. Many Jews continued their business with the farmers outside the town in secrecy. One was Zeev Gritczak, who conducted business with many Polish Christian farmers. Once when Zeev was traveling in his horse and wagon to visit a farmer, a group of young Poles saw him and forced him to stop and get off the wagon. They then beat him up. Fortunately, he was not severely injured and was able to return home.

The Judenrat prepared a list of Jews who could work on projects demanded by the Germans. They assigned Jews to the train station to load and unload coal, weapons, and ammunition. They widened the train tracks. They cut down trees in the nearby forests for firewood. They performed tasks for the municipality, like repairing roads.

The Germans demanded that the Judenrat supply 250 workers for the Dapu railroad workshops in Lapy. This was an enormous railroad car manufacturing facility that became a strategic asset to the Germans.

The work was challenging for those selected. These workers had to get up every morning before dawn and walk to the Kruczewo Train Station by 5:30 a.m. From there, a special train took them to Lapy and their workplaces. At 7:00 p.m., the workers returned home to Sokoly on the same train from the Lapy train station. There was little time to sleep because when workers got home, they had to clean themselves up, eat dinner, prepare food for the next day, and be ready at dawn to start all over again.

One of these workers at Lapy was Rochal Gritczak's brother, Yudel. He was fourteen years old. He did not have to work because of his age, but he volunteered to work in place of his father. As a result, Zeev could continue conducting his leather and fur trading and get money, food, and supplies to support his family. Sheinche also worked at Lapy along with other women. She helped unload trains that held parts and supplies for the manufacturing plant.

On Sunday, November 2, 1941, Yudel went to work. They worked half a day until one o'clock in the afternoon on Sundays. They were then free to leave if they completed their work on time, which they did that day.

The problem was that there was no transportation to Sokoly until six in the evening, so they had to wait at the train station. On their way to the train station, the workers would often go into a Jewish-owned restaurant, the Dworkie Stare Inn, where they could order complete or light meals. The inn was a Jewish trade and smuggling exchange. Trade transactions and commercial agreements were carried out to raise money and goods for the Judenrat.

On that Sunday, ten workers from Sokoly and Bialystok sat in the garden in front of the restaurant, talking with the two young owners.

Suddenly, one worker called out that "Six Feet" was approaching. Six Feet was the nickname of a German military police officer who always traveled with his large German shepherd. Six Feet sought every opportunity and reason to beat and kill Jews. Many times, he beat and killed Jews himself. Other times, he had his dog attack and kill Jews.

When they saw the danger of the unexpected and unwanted encounter, all ten Jews quickly ran to a storage shed behind the restaurant. It was their bad luck that the German saw them running away.

He followed and confronted them inside the shed. They had done nothing wrong. They ran away from him in fear. They were legitimately waiting for the departure of the train. But the German discovered two sacks of flour in the shed, which could only be there through illegal trading.

The owners of the inn denied that the flour belonged to them and said they did not know how the sacks got into the shed. They used this explanation, knowing he would kill them if they had given any other response. Now the door had opened for accusing the ten Jews of smuggling the flour.

Six Feet had the ten Jews taken to a prison camp in the town of Tykocin, where they worked in hard labor. Later, everyone in this work camp was transferred to the Treblinka death camp.

Yudel would never see his parents and sisters again.

My mother told me about Yudel in basic terms. I was shown a

picture of him many years ago. Before I started my research, all I knew was that one day, the Germans took him to a work camp, and the family never saw him again. I knew nothing more. I was heartbroken to learn how my father's uncle and Yudel suffered, their lives taken by two ruthless Germans with dogs.

6

THE GRITCZAKS GO INTO HIDING

B efore conducting my research, I knew that my mother and her family survived the Holocaust by hiding. But that was all I knew.

In late September 1942, the people of Sokoly realized the fate planned for them before liquidation to the death camps began. Reports from neighboring towns and Polish Christians led the inhabitants of Sokoly to understand that Jews from the entire region were being transported to Treblinka, where they were then murdered. Panic set in as they realized the Germans would liquidate Sokoly sometime soon.

In response, a group of youths organized a resistance effort. They met in secret and selected five members for the leadership committee. They developed a plan to set their houses on fire when the Germans announced the liquidation of the town. That would create a distraction, and they could then attack the Germans. They all felt it was better to die after killing even one German than to die in a death camp. They also developed plans for people to flee to the forest and join up with the partisans. They started talking about how to get weapons, food, and supplies.

Unfortunately, their planning began too late. On October 31,

1942, the German commander announced the liquidation of Sokoly would take place the very next day, November 1.

Many individuals, families, and groups developed various plans to flee to the forest. Others had close business relationships with Polish Christian farmers outside of town whom they trusted to hide them in exchange for money because of their friendship. Zeev Gritczak made such arrangements.

Before the liquidation started, people fled to various places. Many got caught in the act and were shot to death. Hundreds of Sokoly Jews escaped to the forest to join the partisans or go into hiding.

Zeev Gritczak and his father, Yaacov, developed many business and personal relationships with the Polish Christians they traded with. They provided loans and personal favors. One, whose last name was Chaikovsky, lived in the village. Yaacov had lent him the money to buy his house without interest. He agreed to help Zeev, but doing so was a significant risk. If caught, Germans would kill the entire families of Poles housing Jews. The Germans were constantly inspecting houses and farms.

Zeev left his two youngest daughters, Rochal, fourteen, and Mina, seven, with the Chaikovsky family. Zeev, Menucha, and Sheinche left for another Polish Christian's farm further away. He told Rochal and Mina to travel from the Chaikovskys' house to this farm on their own after a few days passed. Zeev's parents left Sokoly separately. They traveled from place to place in the forests to hide from the German patrols.

Zeev, Menucha, and Sheinche walked to the Kaponovitchs' farm. He agreed to hide them; Rochal and Mina safely arrived three days later. The family hid in a field of tall wheat and oats at the Kaponovitchs' farm for seven days. If you can imagine hiding in a corn maze, you will get a picture of what hiding in this field was like. Kaponovitch then became concerned about the Germans and getting caught. He told Zeev the family had to leave.

The family left and snuck into a grain silo at another nearby farm. That farmer discovered them. They again had to leave.

They walked to another farm. They saw a grain silo and hid there. They were not detected, so Zeev went to get food and returned. After eleven days, the farmer discovered them and told them to leave.

They traveled about twelve kilometers on foot through the harsh winter to another Christian Zeev knew. They had to walk near a German checkpoint. When they got to the farm, the Christian agreed to hide them. It was a comfortable arrangement but would only last for six weeks. Because the Germans were so close, the nearby partisans would attack the Germans. The gunfire was frightening to the Gritczak sisters, and Zeev left to find another place to stay.

Zeev returned with a Christian farmer from another village on a horse and wagon. Menucha and Mina left on the wagon with the farmer, dressed like Christians. Zeev, Sheinche, and Rochal traveled on foot to a different place. They walked to the farm of another Christian, whose last name was Kroshevsky. Zeev arranged for the entire family to stay in the barn. After three weeks of separation, the family was back together. They would remain there for seventeen months.

In early January, Zeev and Sheinche left to find Zeev's parents, who had left Sokoly separately. They walked through deep snow, and it was bitter cold. They could not find Zeev's parents, so Zeev found a place to stay with a Christian farmer who hid them in his attic. They stayed for a few days so they could get warm and rest. After three days, they left.

They ran into someone they knew while continuing their search. This person told them he had seen Zeev's parents moving around in a specific area, near the home of Chaikovsky, where Zeev's family first stayed. Zeev and Sheinche walked back to the Chaikovskys' house and found his parents there. Polish Christians had taken their shoes and clothing while they were moving around. They appeared very ragged. They had arrived at the Chaikovsky house cold, hungry, and exhausted.

Many Jews who wandered around during this bitter winter could not take it anymore. They traveled back to Sokoly to be captured by the Germans. Zeev's father, Yaacov, decided that this was what he and his wife would do. Zeev tried to convince them to come back with Sheinche and him and join the rest of the family.

Yaacov told his son Zeev, "A rat can cross the street in broad daylight, but if we do so, they will shoot us. There is no point for us to continue. We are too old. We cannot handle the travel, the hiding, the harsh winter conditions. You and your family are young and have a chance to survive and should do so without the burden of us slowing you down."

The next day, Yaacov and his wife, Sarah, left. Sheinche recalls in her testimony watching them through the window as they walked through the deep snow together. She was in tears. Zeev and Sheinche would never see them again.

Later, they heard that Yaacov and Sarah were captured and sent to the Bialystok ghetto. The Germans transported all the Jews of Sokoly to the Bialystok ghetto after liquidation. Later, in November 1943, they liquidated the Bialystok ghetto, transporting all Jews on trains to the Treblinka death camp. A friend of the Gritczaks would escape from Treblinka and later tell them they saw Yaacov, Sarah, and Yudel in Treblinka together, where they died.

Zeev and Sheinche traveled on foot back to the Kroshevsky farm to join Menucha, Rochal, and Mina. They had traveled for six weeks without the rest of the family knowing whether they were alive or not. The family was together again, settling into their life hiding in the barn.

Kroshevsky's oldest daughter would milk the cows daily. One of the empty milk buckets she carried contained potatoes and bread to feed the Gritczak family hiding inside. She did not trigger any suspicions if anyone nearby observed her entering and leaving the barn only when she milked cows. Antisemitic Christians were German collaborators, constantly looking for signs of other Christians helping or hiding Jews. They would turn in fellow Christians for the rewards associated with capturing Jews.

Later, Menucha's niece, Sarah, wandered around in the area

looking for them. She was the daughter of Menucha's sister, who had lived in the mansion. She was aware of many of Zeev's Christian friends. She came to the Kroshevsky farm. They knew her and took her into the barn. Sarah had left her young daughter with a Christian family before she fled. Many Jews did this to save their children. These families would keep them and raise them as Christians. If the parents survived, they would return to get them.

Sarah stayed with the Gritczak family. She would constantly talk about her daughter in despair. Sarah became obsessed and went mad thinking about her daughter, wanting her back. After staying with the Gritczaks for six months, suddenly, one night, she ran away.

Sarah walked back to Sokoly to get her child. She dressed like a Christian and arrived at the church on a Sunday morning. Her plan was to be seen as a Christian and not discovered as a Jew. After the service, she would go to the Christian family's house and get her child back. She was not thinking rationally. Several Christians in the church recognized her and reported it to the Germans. The Germans then killed Sarah, her daughter, and the family that took in her daughter.

Word of this incident got to the Kroshevsky family and scared them. They feared the Germans would try to track down Sarah's hiding place. Every time a stranger came by, they were terrified. Then, there was another incident. Another farmer nearby found two young Jewish men living in one of his fields. He took them in, and they helped with the work in the fields. The farmer's wife was eight months pregnant. The Germans were tipped off, and they came to the house and asked if they were hiding any Jews. They said no, and the Germans searched and found the two Jewish men. The Germans killed the farmer, his pregnant wife, and the two Jews. They had three other young children the Germans spared. The children were given to another nearby farmer who took care of them. After this incident, the Kroshevskys became even more terrified.

In May 1944, Kroshevsky told the Gritczaks he could no longer hide them. He feared they would suffer the same fate as the other farmers. He said he wanted the Gritczaks to commit suicide so that he would not have to kill them. In response, Zeev told him the war was going to end soon. The Russians were already close to the Polish border. Zeev made it clear they would never commit suicide and told Kroshevsky he was a good person, not a killer. Because of their long friendship, Zeev genuinely believed Kroshevsky could never take another person's life.

For a few days, nothing more happened. Then, Kroshevsky came into the barn one early morning and told the Gritczaks that he heard the Germans were coming to search for Jews the following day. He said he had a hiding place in the woods near one of his fields where the Germans would not find them. He had a potato storage pit dug into the ground at this location. The plan was for them to climb into the pit. He would then cover them with enough dirt to not get detected. After the Germans were out of the area, he would get them out of the pit and bring them back to the barn. He would also bring them food every morning. The Gritczaks believed him.

In all their time of hiding, they had walked little and sat most of the time. When the Gritczaks got up and started walking, all five of them had difficulty. Their legs were stiff, and their muscles did not work right. They saw long thick sticks lying on the ground that made good walking sticks along the way. Menucha picked up five sticks so everyone could use one.

When they arrived at the pit, they all climbed into it with their sticks. Kroshevsky took his shovel and started covering them with dirt. As he kept throwing dirt on them, he sounded distraught, crying and saying "oy" repeatedly. He had them covered with dirt and kept on shoveling more into the pit. He would not stop. They then realized he intended to bury them and kill them. They started yelling at him to stop, to no avail.

Now totally buried, they had a hard time breathing. There was no air coming through the dirt above. At first, the family panicked. Then they started poking the soil above them with their sticks. Soon, they created one small opening for air. They then spent most of that day using the sticks to open a hole big enough to crawl out. They used the sticks as support to climb out.

They sat under some nearby trees for the entire night, too afraid to go to sleep. In the morning, Kroshevsky came back to the pit. He did not bring any food, confirming his intent. When he saw them sitting under the tree, he stopped in shock. He took off his boots, started hitting his head with them, and cried. He said he now wanted to take his own life because he would die anyhow because of the Gritczaks. He was afraid of them staying, and he was afraid of them leaving. Finally, after his emotional outburst, he settled down and convinced them to stay.

Things were okay for a few weeks, and then Kroshevsky's fears came back. The Gestapo were making regular raids on houses and farms in the area. One day, he locked the barn so the Gritczaks could not get out. He told them he was going to hang them. He started building the gallows. Zeev realized the danger and escaped through a hole in the barn. He knew he had to act before the gallows were completed. Zeev returned that night with goods and money. He offered it all to Kroshevsky, who accepted it and stopped building the gallows. But this lasted just a few days, and the Gritczaks sensed Kroshevsky would crack again and try to kill them. The Gritczak family left and hid in a wheat field.

Kroshevsky must have been going through an incredible emotional tug of war. He wanted to do the right thing and help the Gritczaks, but he put his family at significant risk. If caught, they would all be killed. As I discovered these details, all I could think about was the absolute emotional hell he must have been experiencing. How could anyone in this situation figure out the right thing to do? Placing family first is why so many Poles turned Jews in or killed them before turning them in. Here was someone trying to do the right thing to save a Jewish family, knowing his own family could be killed.

Zeev Gritczak understood that Kroshevsky was a good person. Zeev understood the farmer's dilemma of saving the Gritczaks and having his own family killed. Therefore, Zeev and the Gritczaks continued to stay there even after the burial and gallows attempts. Through it all, they saw Kroshevsky as a good man, going through hell himself. They would return to his farm for protection after the Russian liberation despite fleeing from him. Zeev never wavered from his friendships, even among Christians.

The family did not have food, clothing, or water when they hid in the wheat field. They were hungry and cold. Russians were making fast progress in their invasion of Poland. Soon, the Gritczaks heard frequent shooting. But their situation got worse. Between the war coming closer to them in one direction and the threat of the Germans still there in the other, they had to remain in hiding with no ability to get food and supplies. They collected water from the rain. They ran out of food, their clothing was soaked in mud, and they had no enclosed shelter.

Rochal was sixteen. She had freckles on her face and exceptionally long hair. When her hair was braided, she looked like a Polish shikse (Yiddish for non-Jewish female).

So, Rochel's hair remained braided. She would travel to local towns in the evenings, appearing as a hungry, cold young Polish Christian girl. She would beg for food and clothing. Her disguise was successful. But she was always in danger of being discovered as a Jew and killed on the spot.

This part of the story was painful when I discovered it. All I could think about was how brave my mother was. I sat at my desk trying to imagine how terrified she must have been each time she went out for food and clothing. I cannot imagine that kind of fear and terror in a sixteen-year-old girl. I also cannot imagine the hell Zeev was going through, having to subject his daughter to these dangerous missions so the entire family could survive. Her mother, Menucha, and sisters did not know if they would ever see her again.

One day, the Gritczaks were all sitting in the wheat field. German soldiers appeared. Everyone in the family ran in different directions. They had an agreed-upon wheat field to meet in once everyone felt safe. Three days later, they all returned to that field. One night, they walked to a different wheat field where they saw a group of antisemitic Polish partisans who would kill them if discovered. They ran and hid in a bunker they found. In the morning, one Polish partisan came by and opened the bunker. They were trapped. The Gritczaks recognized this partisan from Sokoly. He, too, knew them.

Zeev suddenly jumped out of the bunker, ran, and escaped. He did not intend to abandon his family. He intended to leave an obvious message to this Pole that if he did anything to harm his family, he was out there to return and track him down. This Pole also knew that Zeev was well-known and liked, even by Christians. The war was almost over, and back in Sokoly, he would not stand a chance with other Poles if Zeev came after him. The Pole let them go. Zeev knew what he was doing, and he did not return for three weeks. He had stayed with a Christian friend in another village and accumulated money and food. The family worried about him for those three weeks. They thought he had been captured or killed. But he was safe.

Zeev had a natural ability to connect with other people, including Christians, and trade with them wherever he went. He was also a quiet man who did not talk a lot. He often assumed people knew what he was thinking. His family, in this case, had no clue of what he was thinking. But it worked.

Three weeks later, the family traveled on the main road when they ran into a group of Russians and Jewish partisans. When the Gritczaks spoke in Yiddish, the Jewish partisans were overjoyed. The partisans told them they had to get out of the area. The Russian army was advancing and would come through this road soon. The Gritczaks headed back to the Kroshevskys, whose farm was nearby. The Kroshevskys welcomed them.

The Russians soon liberated the Bialystok and Sokoly areas. The Germans moved further west as the Russian army kept advancing. The war was still on until the fall of Berlin. But for the Sokoly and Bialystok region, the war was over. The German threat no longer existed. Still, the danger to Jews was far from over.

Kroshevsky barn in 1989. The Gritczak family hid here for seventeen months.

In 1989, my aunt Sheinche asked my mother to join her on a trip to Poland. My mother said she would never go back there. Sheinche traveled with her son Avi and daughter Sarah. They met the children and grandchildren of the Kroshevskys. The now elderly children remembered her and welcomed them.

Rochal Gritczak with her braided hair after liberation, 1944.

7

PRUZHANY JUDENRAT

A myth prevails that the Judenrats were corrupt collaborators with the Germans. Survivors universally disagree with that. Most Judenrats consisted of honest, caring leaders. They were selected to make the best out of a terrible situation. Yes, there were a few examples of corrupt Judenrats, but they were not the norm. This myth comes from confusion in interchanging Jewish ghettos with the death camps. The Jewish leaders (kapos) were corrupt collaborators selected by the Germans in the death camps. The Jews had no say in their selection nor in the work they performed. In the ghettos, the Jewish community selected the Judenrat members. The Judenrat managed the affairs of the ghetto on behalf of the Jewish residents.

The Judenrat of Pruzhany had twenty-four members. They did their work exceptionally well. They were the gold standard of serving selflessly for the greater good. Not only was there no greed, there was also no corruption or collaboration with the Gestapo. They were the strongest leaders and experts in the Jewish community. Every member of the Pruzhany Judenrat focused on saving Jews, making their lives in the ghetto as comfortable as possible, and minimizing German terror. They were brilliant in managing every demand and situation for the benefit of all. The Pruzhany Judenrat enhanced the life of its Jewish citizens under the worst of circumstances.

In July 1941, the Germans ordered the Jewish population of Pruzhany to collect two kilograms of gold, ten kilograms of silver, 500,000 rubles, one hundred pairs of shoes, and one hundred fur coats within a day. Other Jewish communities also asked the Pruzhany Judenrat for help. They needed help paying their mandated contribution to the Germans, which they had no means to pay. The Pruzhany Judenrat agreed to help. The Pruzhany Jewish community donated their possessions and candlesticks and candelabras from the synagogue to collect the required sum. People gave whatever was needed to satisfy the Germans. They knew what the alternative meant for the entire community.

Later in July, the Gestapo's commander summoned the Judenrat team and ordered them to establish a ghetto for the Jews of Pruzhany. The Judenrat received the plan and the barbed wire fence specifications. The Judenrat had to supply the labor to build the fence.

In September 1941, they completed building the ghetto. All the Jews who lived outside the ghetto had to move from their houses to the ghetto area. Christians who lived within the ghetto boundaries had to move out.

The Germans rumored that Pruzhany and the surrounding region would become a "Judenshtat" (Jewish state) where all the Jews of Europe would eventually live. They annexed Belarus as part of German Prussia. It was now considered the territory of the Third Reich.

At the same time the Germans treated the nearby Bialystok region differently. The Bialystok region was not annexed. However, the Germans took over the direct administration of the Bialystok region as if it were part of Belarus for economic reasons to support the war effort.

The city of Bialystok was the center of a large economic region. Much of Poland's industrial base was in this area.

Pruzhany was 144 kilometers from Bialystok. This industrial base became a major Supply Center for the German army. It was impossible to operate all the region's factories without the Jews. The Jews were a large part of the skilled workers, artisans, and specialists working in these industries.

All the other areas occupied by Germany kept their identities as separate countries without direct German administration. Jews in Belarus and the Bialystok region were told their lives would be better under the administration of the Third Reich than the Jews who lived in these other "bandit, hoodlum countries." Like the Jews in Germany who were used for labor, the Jews of the Bialystok region would perform work for the Third Reich and pay the taxes demanded of them. If the Jews supplied what they required of them, they would not meet the fate of the Jews outside the Third Reich.

The ghettos in this region were operated differently than the more tightly controlled prison camps in other areas. While the ghettos were fenced in and secured, Jews regularly traveled outside the ghettos for work. The Judenrats were given much more authority and flexibility as long as they provided the labor and anything else the Germans demanded.

This mutually beneficial arrangement did delay the fate of the Jews in this region. Many began to believe the German lie that they would not be sent to death camps. However, once the Germans no longer needed the Jewish labor, these communities were liquidated and sent to death camps.

The creation of Judenshtat never happened. Two thousand Jews from Bialystok were transferred to Pruzhany and another two thousand from other villages. After this, the Germans stopped sending additional Jews to Pruzhany.

The strategy changed. In the early years of the war, the plan was to move all Jews into Judenshtat, where they would be totally segregated from the rest of Europe. At that time their destiny would be decided. In other words, Judenshtat was envisioned to be a "storage facility" for Jews until their final fate could be determined. Then the "Final Solution" became the strategy. The

Final Solution called for building massive death camps for the sole purpose of the mass extermination of Jews. For the first time in history, industrial methods were used to exterminate an entire people. The Jews could now be quickly annihilated. There was no longer a need for Judenshtat.

From that point on, the Jewish ghettos and movement of Jews became focused on the most efficient hubs to transport Jews to the death camps. Bialystok became the region's central ghetto and collection point for Jews as their towns were liquidated. From there, they were sent to the death camps in large groups daily.

The Judenrat had to carry out everything the Germans demanded. Many times, they did not know the task they had to execute. They provided the Germans with large numbers of workers to work in places arranged in advance. The Judenrat decided which workers to assign for each job. The work included clearing snow, cutting wood, forest clearing, home servants, loading and repairing guns and ammunition, earthworks, and more. Craft workers were engaged in shoemaking, sewing, and furniture making. The Germans imposed heavy taxes on the Jews. The Judenrat had to collect the fines among the Jews of Pruzhany: gold, silver, furs, boots, whatever it took. The rich had to give more because the poor had nothing to offer. If the Judenrat supplied everything demanded, the community seemed to survive.

The Judenrat managed daily life and affairs in the ghetto. They supplied the police and security for the Jewish population. They always had to balance the demands of the Germans with what was possible to carry out.

The German authorities lived in and ran their command offices in the Christian part of town. They assigned Jews to work in that part of town. As a result, they met the peasants often and began a secret underground trade that the Judenrat managed strategically. One could get food for a piece of material or leather, which was in high demand. The underground economy became the solution for hunger, and a means to gain goods for bribes.

The Judenrat received payments for the workers requested by the Germans, but it was not enough. It was necessary to collect a tax from the Pruzhany Jews from time to time. The Judenrat also used several illegal methods to increase its income, such as trading contraband.

Workshops in the ghetto solved many problems and needs. People working at these workshops constructed furniture, sewed clothing, performed carpentry, and made shoes. They made baked goods and distilled whiskey. Clothes, boots, and whiskey became the best items to bribe the Germans. The Germans brought leather and wood, and Jews made shoes and furniture. When some material was leftover, they used it to make items for the ghetto.

Organizing the workshops did not take long. The Judenrat gained both work tools and materials through "nationalizations." All possessions of the ghetto residents became community property. The Judenrat managed everything for the collective good.

Shmeryl Elman was assigned to a detail when the four thousand Jews from Bialystok and other towns arrived at the train station. The Germans had farmers bring trucks, horses, and wagons to the train station to bring these people to the ghetto. Shmeryl would help direct people to a truck or wagon and help them get in with their belongings. He had a tough job because Germans and Poles, in large numbers, came to the train station when these trains arrived. Their sole purpose was to beat the arriving Jews with bats and sticks as they got off the trains and walked to the trucks and wagons. Shmeryl and the others worked as fast as possible to shield them and minimize the beatings.

During this time, Yossel was assigned to work at the airport. The jobs varied and involved unloading weapons and ammunition left by the Russians, unloading German planes that flew in, and other tasks. The winters in that region were very harsh. There was a lot of snow and bitterly cold temperatures. They assigned hundreds of Jews to clear the snow at the airport using shovels and wheelbarrows. If they worked too slowly, they would be beaten with sticks and whips.

As fate would have it, the Elman family had to take in other people that arrived from other towns into their homes. One was Eliezer Shayn, who came to visit Pruzhany only a few days before the German occupation. He could not leave. Eliezer spoke fluent German and proved himself to be a go-between with the Germans. He had strong organizational, leadership, and negotiating skills and became an invaluable member of the ghetto. During the formation of the Judenrat, they asked him to be a member because everyone had high regard for him. Later, the Elmans had to vacate their house and move in with their grandparents. Eliezer moved in with another family.

The German Burger Meister (mayor) of Pruzhany asked the Judenrat to provide a house servant for the house he occupied with his wife. The Judenrat viewed this as an opportunity to place someone who could do that job exceptionally well and earn the trust of the mayor and his wife. The person had to be discreet and savvy enough to provide information on conversations and activities inside the mayor's house. If successful, they would have a Jewish spy within the home of the Burger Meister.

Eliezer Shayn convinced the Judenrat that Shmeryl Elman was the right person for this dangerous job. Any missteps could lead to being shot on the spot. Eliezer spoke with Shmeryl, and he accepted with no hesitation. They then moved him from the train station group to the mayor's house.

Shmeryl was responsible for all the provisions in the mayor's house. Every morning, he would walk to the ghetto gate with his pass, grab a bicycle provided to him, and ride to the mayor's house. After work, he would ride the bike back and reenter the ghetto. In the winter, Shmeryl had to walk. The mayor had many meetings, dinners, parties, and private discussions with his wife. Shmeryl could overhear most of what was said. He listened to the radio in the house for outside news. Shmeryl would then share relevant information with the Judenrat.

The mayor's wife liked Shmeryl and was kind to him. She sometimes gave him food, firewood, and other items to take home to his family. The mayor was also very civil with Shmeryl.

The people of Pruzhany did not suffer from hunger in the

ghetto even though the Germans intended that hunger would be prevalent in all Jewish ghettos. Survival instincts create ingenuity in all people. An underground economy thrived across all Jewish ghettos, involving Jews and Christians. The Judenrat was able to supply food for the workers sent to work outside the ghetto and the workshop workers inside the ghetto. They provided for those ill at the hospital and children at kindergarten. They opened free kitchens and dining places for the homeless. Jews who could provide themselves with food did not receive any from the Judenrat.

The Judenrat managed and gained much more food than the Germans officially allocated. They received and handled all contraband food items. Jews working outside the ghetto were in touch with Christians and could buy from them. Christians often got special permission to enter the ghetto and asked the Jewish shoemakers to make their shoes and boots. The same happened with Jewish tailors. They got paid for this work. They also set up channels to move goods outside the ghetto to sell or trade. Smuggling became a daily activity.

Workers transported the ghetto's garbage to a dump on the outskirts of town. The workers then put products into the garbage baskets to be smuggled back to the ghetto.

The fire brigade for all Pruzhany was located inside the ghetto. Jewish firefighters had to extinguish fires in the non-Jewish area, too. They filled their vehicles with items needed for life in the ghetto on their way back.

The Germans did not provide the Judenrat with any bread. The flour and mills were outside the ghetto. Traveling to and from the mills allowed the Jews to trade with the Christian population for needed goods. They hid those goods in the flour and then "legally" brought the flour into the ghetto.

The Judenrat received the officially assigned quantities of goods through the mayor. He provided a supply form for the Supply Center. The Supply Center was a central warehouse managed by the Germans that distributed goods to the German authorities living in Pruzhany and the Jewish ghetto. They bribed the German and Polish officers to supply more than the mayor allowed at the Supply Center. The same happened with the mills. There, the officers received bribes to get extra flour.

The Judenrat had the right to send its doctors to poor homes, even if these people could not pay. Everyone, without exception, received the same medical help as those who could pay for it. However, getting medicines and drugs was difficult. There were no pharmacies in the ghetto. So, the hospital staff had to pay costly prices to get medication and drugs through illegal channels.

Bribery became an essential means to protect the Jews in the ghetto from German harm. The Judenrat had to bribe German and Polish guards at the ghetto gates. They had to bribe German officials. They successfully bribed the Lehman Bandits to be less brutal toward Jews.

Bribes also helped reverse German decrees that would place great hardship in the ghetto. The bribes, together with meeting all the demands of the Germans, stopped the beatings, looting, and killing of Jews.

The Judenrat of Pruzhany performed miracles to benefit all the Jews in the ghetto. In the end, all twenty-four members were part of the German liquidation of the ghetto. Only two survived Auschwitz. They were righteous people to the very end.

Most images of Holocaust history do not separate life in the ghettos from life in the death camps. In the ghettos, the goal of the Germans was to keep Jews confined. They allowed what went on inside the ghetto to be managed by Jews. All the Germans wanted was their demands met. On the other hand, the death camps were more like a prison. The Germans controlled the perimeter of the camps and everything inside. The Jews were worked and starved to death before going to the gas chambers.

In the ghettos, the Jews used their skills and ingenuity to make life as comfortable as possible under terrible circumstances. The Germans expected starvation and disease to overcome the ghettos. The Jews fought back by creating underground economies, trading with Christians who needed goods only Jews could supply. They used bribes to get cooperation from guards. They minimized the death and destruction of Jews inside the ghettos. The Judenrats made the Germans feel comfortable and in control while they smoothly managed the internal affairs of the ghettos. This German hands-off approach allowed them to conduct illegal activities without getting caught. They kept the Germans ignorant of the actual activities underway in the ghettos. Unfortunately, there is little documentation of ghetto life through pictures. I could not find any images of ghetto life and activities in my research.

On the other hand, the death camps were very well documented with pictures. So, those pictures get used interchangeably to represent both the death camps and ghettos. The resistance in the ghettos can only be explained verbally.

I am in absolute awe of how the Jews controlled their lives inside the ghetto and set the foundation for people to escape and survive. The stories of every ghetto are remarkably similar. If not for the Judenrat and the industries and economy set up inside the ghettos, the ability to have adequate food, clothing, housing, and medical treatment would never have existed. The ability to collect weapons, ammunition, and supplies for those to flee would never have been possible. And the coordination and communication established with Russian partisans would never have happened. Before my research, I had no idea about the complexities of the ghettos or the role of the Judenrat. The real story of the ghettos is about ingenuity and bravery, which could have forever gone undocumented, swallowed by the tragedies of the Holocaust.

The largest Jewish uprising is well documented but is still not well-known. Warsaw was the largest city in Poland. Its Jewish ghetto was also the largest. In 1940, the ghetto contained 400,000 Jews. By early 1943, only about 75,000 remained.

On April 19, 1943, the Germans announced the ghetto's liquidation. The Warsaw ghetto uprising then began. The fighters forced the Germans to retreat for a brief time. Then more German troops entered the ghetto with tanks and heavy artillery. They again were forced to pull back.

About seven hundred Jewish resistance fighters, armed with a small cache of weapons and support from the rest of the Jewish population, managed to fight off the Germans for a month. The Germans, forced to retreat several times, finally brought in thousands of additional troops and heavy weapons and crushed the uprising. The entire ghetto was destroyed. While the Jews never expected to win, holding off the German army for a month demonstrated that the Germans were not invincible. This event also made the Germans fear that the Jews did have the ability to fight back fiercely. The Warsaw ghetto uprising became a catalyst for similar uprisings in other Jewish ghettos.

On December 16, 1943, an uprising began in the Bialystok ghetto. The Jews held off the Germans for four days. These resistance stories belong among other events of Jews overcoming adversity throughout our history. The fight to survive inside the ghettos and the uprisings belong in Jewish history together with events like Massada, Purim, Hannukah, the Spanish Inquisition, and more.

I leave this topic with mixed emotions. I feel pride and admiration for the bravery and ingenuity of the Jews in the ghettos. The Jews had no chance once they were sent to the death camps without outside help, which never came. The allied command knew about the death camps and did not consider them "strategic targets" to bomb and destroy. How could the mass production facilities that killed millions of Jews and others not be considered strategic to stop? Many of the death camps were close to other weapons and manufacturing sites the allies did bomb. The true answers to this will never be known. We can only speculate.

8

ORGANIZING THE PRUZHANY
PARTISANS

I n Pruzhany, the Judenrat did its best to avoid any mass action of partisan organizing. They knew that any gatherings or activities in large numbers would at once gain the attention of the Germans and result in retaliation, even the destruction of the entire Pruzhany ghetto. They believed that if things remained calm and under control, they could continue their successful effort to keep the ghetto functioning and safe for the Jewish inhabitants.

In the spring of 1942, two formal underground groups were established inside the ghetto. Aron Goldstein, Yossef Rosen, and Yitzhak Shereshevsky led one. Yitzhak Frydberg and Shmeryl Elman led the other. Small groups escaped to the forest and connected with Russian partisans. Ten set up a camp in the forest to store weapons, food, and supplies in anticipation of many fleeing the ghetto. Some of the weapons and supplies were provided to Russian partisans aiding them. People traveled back and forth from the ghetto and forest to coordinate activities inside and outside the ghetto. Yossel traveled back and forth several times.

In the fall of 1942, they heard the Germans were liquidating towns and Jewish ghettos near Pruzhany. These towns were also under the control of the Third Reich. This information confirmed that being under the Third Reich's control only put these towns at the end of the list for liquidation. The eventual liquidation of the Pruzhany ghetto was a certainty. The best they could do was to continue to delay the inevitable.

Yossel Elman joined Shmeryl in organizing the underground inside the ghetto. Their father, a pessimist, told them they were just wasting their time. He was extremely negative and depressed, believing everyone would end up in death camps. He told his sons they had nowhere to escape, as the Germans occupied the countries in every direction they could go. Their father also told them a Jewish man could never hide or conceal his identity from the Germans. All they had to do was pull down their pants, and they would at once know they were Jews.

Their mother did not encourage them or discourage them. She knew that staying would lead them to the death camps. Fleeing would also likely result in death. It was their choice to make.

Yitzhak Frydberg managed the selection and assignment of all Jewish workers requested by the Germans for the Judenrat. He also led the workers who worked in the forests, cutting down trees for firewood. While in the woods, Yitzhak ran into some Russian partisans one day. The Russians needed more fighters and asked Yitzhak and his group to join them. Yitzhak told them they could not flee now and risk the lives of the Judenrat and the rest of the people in the ghetto. He said that small groups of young men would organize and join them in the forest in time. A critical connection with the Russian partisans now existed.

Connecting with Russian partisan groups was critical for Jews who fled. There was significant antisemitism in partisan groups, especially those with Belarusian, Polish, Lithuanian, Ukrainian, and others in command or in large numbers. Such groups deliberately killed many Jewish partisans.

The Jews from all towns and cities that made it to the forest were also sought out by Christian peasants living nearby. Most peasants in the villages were antisemitic and would alert the Germans to their whereabouts if detected. The Germans also had patrols in the area searching for Jews. Finding Russian partisans became the priority for all Jews who fled to the forest.

While Russians were antisemitic, Stalin viewed the partisan effort as critical to defeating the Germans. He ordered through his chain of command that any antisemitism was not tolerated and would be subjected to punishment. Stalin had no sympathy for Jews. His focus was pushing the Germans back with whatever it took, including Jews.

Even if they did reach the Russian partisan groups, Jews still faced many difficulties. A substantial number were unarmed and without supplies. Weapons were usually a minimum requirement to join a Russian partisan group unless an individual had some other strategic experience a group needed. Many Jews fled with their families but taking in families was risky to the Russian partisans for many reasons.

The first people to escape to the forest and join the Russian partisans were an orphan brought up in Pruzhany and his wife. They set the path for others who began doing the same. Small groups tried to escape. Some got past the German guards at the fence who shot at them.

The Jews of Pruzhany who successfully made it into the forest made their way to the Russian partisans expecting them. Jews from other towns also engaged with the Russians. People moved back and forth between the Pruzhany ghetto and the forest to coordinate between the partisan group and the organizing youth in the ghetto.

Yossel Elman moved back and forth along with others. Shmeryl's focus was on helping to organize things inside the ghetto. As more people in the ghetto escaped, more people became encouraged to flee. But they needed to have weapons, proper clothing, food, and items for bribing guards. To get these resources, they had to work with the Judenrat. They had to be incredibly careful and only talk to those who needed to know. The youth took the advice of the Judenrat to only go to the forest one by one or in small groups. The agreement was that people would only gather and flee in large numbers if the liquidation of the ghetto were to begin—at that point, there would be nothing to lose.

The Germans sensed that something was going on. They increased the number of guards and paid more attention to day-to-day activities. On the morning of November 1, 1942, German guards surrounded the entire ghetto perimeter without warning. No Jews could leave the ghetto. Shmeryl Elman walked to the ghetto gate to get his bicycle and ride it to work. The bike was not there. The guards told him to go home. No one could leave, not even for work.

The Gestapo commander told the Judenrat that the ghetto would be evacuated within days or weeks. He said the Jews would go to work camps, and no harm would come to them. The Judenrat now had to begin preparations according to German orders. Horses and wagons would take them to the train station for transport. The Germans were developing a list of names and the schedules for when they had to show up for transport.

While the Germans claimed they were being sent to work camps, the Jews knew what this meant. A few days later, a group of about forty physicians, teachers, attorneys, and other professionals tried to perform a collective suicide. They all gathered at one home, took morphine, and lit a fire in the fireplace. They closed the fireplace damper and shut all the windows. All of them passed out. But several neighbors, including an aunt of the Elman brothers, smelled smoke and ran to the house. They saw the house filled with smoke, then entered, opened the windows, and dragged them out. All but one recovered.

Another forty-seven people, including Shmeryl and Yossel Elman's father, committed suicide individually as the Jews of the ghetto waited for their eventual fate. The people who committed suicide could not bear to see their families taken to the death camps. They took their own lives to deny that to the Germans.

My father kept a diary of his experiences. (The original diary was written in Yiddish and translated by others.) Reading this entry brought me to tears:

> *My father was hanging, his feet still moving. I walked back to the house, opened the door, and told them to give me a knife! Everybody looked at me, surprised. I took the knife, returned to the grain warehouse, and then cut the rope.*
>
> *I come home, carrying on my shoulder the dead body of my warm and beloved father. He ended his life not to see the way his wife and children would be annihilated. My mother fainted. My sisters and younger brother fell silent. They couldn't say a single word. The responsibility of taking care of the family was now on me. With what ease my father (bless his memory) carried out his execution! All premeditated to avoid the torture of the Germans, and he achieved it! He was better off than us now. His life was finished while we were still feeling the slaughter.*

Binyamin Elman could not overcome the emotional torture of the dilemma he faced. He could not sit still and do nothing to protect his family. At the same time, he knew that if he took any action to protect his family and got caught, the Germans would kill the whole family as collective punishment. For him, taking his own life was the only way out of this dilemma. The pain and horror my father and his family experienced with Binyamin's suicide, also knowing they too were facing certain death, is incomprehensible. And this was only the beginning of a long journey of miracles and hell for all of them.

Binyamin Elman shortly before he committed suicide

The following are all of my father's diary entries from November 1942:

November 1, 1942

The ghetto is closed. Our time has come. As soon as we turn around, we meet the cold and murderous faces of the German guards around the ghetto. The atmosphere is strained. People are running up and down the streets like poisoned rats, not knowing what to do. Everyone could see his end getting closer, the ghetto's end, but everyone wanted to live!

The youth groups were meeting at several points near the ghetto's fences. Everyone wanted to save himself, but they were out of strength and spirit. Gestapo is going around in vehicles on the ghetto's streets, getting ready for the sad end. Thousands of dead who are still alive, but who know every minute they could be killed, crawl by the streets and hope for a miracle. Only a miracle could save the thousands of people that were later annihilated through horrible suffering, just because of their Jewish names.

The Gestapo chief came to the Judenrat and told them every Jew must be ready for the liquidation. It will take place in one day or two weeks. One thing is sure: the liquidation will happen, and everyone must be ready. This statement makes the blood freeze in the veins.

Some youth groups have organized for resistance, but the Judenrat committee begged them to be calm and wait so they may reverse the sanction. The youth wait for the night. In this atmosphere, a day goes by. At night, the Germans reinforce the guard. Around the ghetto, they have installed electric spotlights. Every minute spotlights surround the ghetto's fences.

The groups meet near the fences until the rifle's bullets break up the meeting people, leaving some dead and injured. Others resigned themselves not to attempt escape and withdraw. The frequent bullet explosions are the motivation for those of us who longed for escape.

November 2, 1942

The same atmosphere. Seeing it was impossible to escape from the ghetto, people dug underground bunkers. It was like an epidemic. Young and older men, everyone dug defense bunkers. They collected food in the way everyone could. Still, we knew what our destiny would be: to be discovered by the Germans, specialists in death. Everyone thinks maybe his destiny isn't to be found. Some try again to escape, but they fall after being shot near the ghetto's fence.

November 3, 1942

The delay in the liquidation makes the people feel calm, although they know it's impossible to save themselves. Frequently, Germans arrive in their trucks, creating a war of nerves. Many lose their mind. Social institutions get calmed. It all goes to show the end is appointed.

November 4, 1942

In the ghetto, starting early morning, a crowd of Christians has gathered in front of the ghetto's fence. They wait for the blood to spread to begin to get the spoils. The Jew is thought of as impure, but his goods are acceptable. The human feeling in the Christians gathered here is something from the past. That's why their eyes are sparkling like beasts in their run after the spoils. Hearts explode while seeing these beasts moving freely, and a people of such a beautiful tradition are being wildly annihilated. That's the way days pass. The half-dead are exhausted, nerves are out of control, many commit suicide.

Shmeryl's diary notes from November 5 to 12 cannot be found. During that time, the liquidation of Jews had still not started.

November 13, 1942

In the ghetto now. Early morning, it's rumored that the Germans have already evacuated the Jews of Blesk to the camps. When I get home, I learn my father hasn't been there for breakfast, and our family is looking for him everywhere. My mother was distraught and didn't find a comfortable place at home. My brother and I don't have time for these "little things." We made up our minds to give up our precious lives, but, for as long as it was possible, we wanted to survive so we could take revenge on those who spread our blood.

Although it's impossible now to leave the ghetto, it was possible to wait for the liquidation in the underground bunkers and then go to the forest. Doing this was stupid for my parents, but we worked very hard to achieve it.

At night, my sister turned up, crying and running to our bunker. She asked, "Are you here? We're looking for Dad, and we can't find him." My heart misses a beat, and I think he hung himself! I rush outside like a gust of wind. Every place was searched for except the grain warehouse. The grain warehouse was always locked, and only my father had the key. Nobody thought about looking there. Only I did. I got in through the small crack. It's dark inside. A ray of sun comes in through the crack, and it lights a rope hanging from the roof. My father was hanging, his feet still moving. I walked back to the house, opened the door, and told them to give me a knife! Everybody looked at me, surprised. I took the knife, returned to the grain warehouse and then cut the rope.

I come home, carrying on my shoulder the dead body of my warm and beloved father. He ended his life not to see the way his wife and children would be annihilated. My mother fainted. My sisters and younger brother fell silent. They couldn't say a single word. The responsibility of taking care of the family was now on me. With what ease my father (bless his memory) carried out his execution! All premeditated to avoid the torture of the Germans, and he achieved it! He was better off than us now. His life was finished while we were still feeling the slaughter.

The burial took place the next day. The whole town accompanied him and thought he was the happiest of them all.

November 15, 1942

Evening. 14 days have passed, in darkness and tension—14 days of being exposed to death every minute. Then the relief came. The Pruzhany ghetto would stay in place until the springtime of the following year. That's what the killer Nazis decided to do. This news cheered up the living dead. My father wasn't lucky to live for that now. Since I was the oldest boy, I took the responsibility of being the supplier and adviser of my ill-fated family. It was clear to me everything was temporary, and our final day would come, anyway. Our fate would not differ from the thousands of towns and villages that were already annihilated.

Many young men began to think about making weapons and escaping to the woods to join the partisans fighting against the bandits.

After weeks of everyone believing the end was near, the Judenrat convinced the Germans to rescind the order to liquidate the ghetto. Their argument to the Germans was that the Jews of the ghetto directly worked for the German Army and Third Reich. The Jews of Pruzhany were of more value to them alive and continuing this work. The Germans accepted this argument and delayed the liquidation order until spring.

The next day, everyone went back to work, including Shmeryl Elman. The Germans guards were back to their earlier staffing levels. The Judenrat now knew that there would eventually be a day of destruction. Helping the youth escape became their top priority.

In the beginning, it was not clear what the function of the Judenrat "Fight Organization" was. There were different proposals. One was to organize setting the ghetto on fire to throw the Germans into a panic so that the Jews could escape. That was too risky. They focused on preparing small groups at a time to leave. A large-scale escape would only take place when the liquidation of the ghetto began. Then there was nothing to lose.

There were already instances of people escaping every day. The Germans shot many of them, but some made it through to the forest. The Judenrat and the youth planning to escape understood that getting out and joining established partisans was only possible with weapons and provisions. So, obtaining weapons became a top priority.

There were fifty Jews assigned to work daily at the airport. They unloaded the guns and munitions the Russians had left behind. There was also a second location near the airport where Jewish workers repaired broken firearms.

The Judenrat member responsible for organizing the Fight Organization authorized and aided the effort to smuggle guns into the ghetto. They could only smuggle revolvers and metallic rifle pieces. They had to remove the wood stock off all rifles to hide them inside the smugglers' clothing. They would shove the long metal barrels into their shirt and down through their pant legs. They wore very baggy clothing to allow for this. They stuffed compartments sewn into their pants for ammunition. Their shoes had special liners to hide bullets between the insole and sole. They tied grenades to their ankles, covered by their pant legs and socks. They built bunkers to store weapons near the airport and outside the repair facility. They would later smuggle the weapons into the ghetto.

Late at night, in the basement of a Jewish woodworker's home inside the ghetto, they made new rifle wood stocks from scratch. They assembled these stocks on the rifles they had smuggled in.

Other people inside the ghetto dug defense and escape bunkers into the ground. They built most of these in the basements of homes, which all had dirt floors. They constructed other bunkers near the perimeter barbed wire fence of the ghetto as a future staging area for escape. They built these bunkers primitively. They stored food, fuel, matches, white bedsheets, and other supplies for the youth that would escape. Many of these bunkers were so secret and clandestine even their families living above did not know about them.

The biggest challenge was how to get the weapons into the ghetto from the storage bunkers.

The Judenrat started supplying whiskey bottles to the workers at the airport and gun repair facility to bribe and "befriend" the guards. Guards stationed at the ghetto gates received bribes to ease the movement of illegal food and goods in and out of the ghetto. Whiskey was something the guards always wanted. They then looked the other way, paying no attention to the gates.

Soon, the weapons and ammunition were smuggled into the ghetto and hidden in bunkers. Shmeryl Elman coordinated, storing all the weapons and ammunition inside the ghetto.

The Elmans now lived with their aunt, who lost her husband to the dogs of the Lehman Bandits. They moved there after their father committed suicide. The brothers built a large bunker in the basement of their aunt's house to store all the weapons.

There was still a problem with moving the weapons stored at the repair facility into the ghetto, as that was in a more difficult area to smuggle things through. But it turned out the repair facility was near the Burger Meister's house. Shmeryl Elman traveled every day to and from that house. It was now winter and freezing. Shmeryl developed a plan to smuggle those weapons into the ghetto.

The plan was for Shmeryl to use a special sled with a hidden compartment to pick up the guns. They would place firewood on top of the sled. He would use the kindness of the mayor's wife to help him.

On the morning of the weapons pickup, Shmeryl walked to the ghetto gate with the specially built wood sled. After the guards checked the sled, he then walked out the gate. Shmeryl arrived at the mayor's house, leaving the sled outside.

Once inside the house, he saw the mayor's wife and approached her. Shmeryl told her that the last few nights had been frigid in his home, and his mother was ill. He asked if she would provide firewood that he could take home with him. He explained that he brought a sled for this purpose. She agreed and told him he could take as much as he needed. He told her he would load the sled at the end of the day and thanked her.

At lunchtime, Shmeryl left the house to go pick up the guns. He grabbed the sled and headed over to the repair facility with it. Meantime, the workers at the repair facility brought whiskey with them that morning and gave it to the guards. They told the guards that a friend was stopping by during lunch to pick up firewood that they would load on the sled at the gate. The guards said okay. They then got the guns out of the bunker and wrapped them. They placed the wrapped guns on a regular sled and hid them. They were now ready for Shmeryl's arrival.

Shmeryl was in a dangerous situation, walking the sled toward the repair facility. He was walking in the opposite direction of the ghetto. The work permit he carried did not allow him to be in that area. He walked with the sled, his yellow Jude Star visible to all, not knowing if anyone would stop him and question him. He knew he could be shot for being where he did not belong.

Fortunately, no one interfered, and he made it to the gate of the repair facility. He also had some whiskey. He told the guards he was there to pick up firewood from some friends and gave them the whiskey. The guards walked inside to drink it. The other workers saw Shmeryl and quickly came over with their sled and the firewood on it.

They placed the guns in the secret compartment of Shmeryl's sled. A board was nailed on top, and a blanket covered it. They stacked firewood on top, and Shmeryl then tied it down.

Shmeryl returned to the mayor's house to complete his afternoon of work. He parked the sled and went back into the home to work. When his work was complete in the early evening, he told the mayor's wife that he was leaving and would load the firewood on the sled and head home.

It was frigid and dark. The mayor had a chauffeur and traveled in a Mercedes, except during winter, when he traveled with a horse and carriage to get through the snow, ice, and rough roads. The mayor's wife said she did not want Shmeryl walking home in such cold and dark weather. She offered to have the chauffeur take him and the sled back to his home in the ghetto. Shmeryl gladly accepted her kind offer and thanked her.

He walked outside, adding as much wood as possible over the existing wood, and tied it all down. The chauffeur tied the sled behind the wagon. Shmeryl sat next to the chauffeur as they traveled to the ghetto. They passed through the gate and stopped at his aunt's house. Shmeryl untied the sled and thanked the chauffeur. Yossel was waiting, knowing Shmeryl was coming home with the guns. He helped load the weapons into the bunker in the basement. The Germans never knew the mayor's chauffeur inadvertently brought the weapons into the ghetto.

Shmeryl would use the sled several more times to smuggle weapons. The chauffeur only helped with the sled the one time. All other times Shmeryl pulled the sled back with him.

Guns alone were not enough to survive as a partisan. Shoemakers made boots. Tailors made unique clothing. They also obtained food, tools, and other supplies and stored them for this effort.

The focus was to prepare as many young people as possible to flee the ghetto in small groups and join the partisans. If the Germans were to announce and begin the liquidation of the ghetto, organized groups would leave in large numbers as fast as possible. The Judenrat managed the distribution of all weapons, food, and supplies inside the ghetto as people prepared to join the partisans. This effort went smoothly.

The youth organizing their escape kept their word to minimize exposure and formed small groups of ten to fifteen. They understood the risk to the Judenrat and the whole ghetto if caught. Jews from Pruzhany already lived in the forest with established Russian partisans. Two or three traveled back and forth between the Pruzhany ghetto and forest. Meetings took place inside the ghetto to plan the movement of people, weapons, and supplies to support the growing number of Jewish and

Russian partisans already organized in the forest. Shmeryl and Yossel participated in many of these discussions.

On the evening of January 27, 1943, all hell broke loose. Two partisans came back into the ghetto to meet with the Judenrat in their offices. The intent was to further coordinate the movement of clothes, supplies, and weapons into the forest.

The partisans and the chief of the Gestapo arrived at the Judenrat offices almost simultaneously. The chief entered and saw the two armed partisans. He drew his weapon and started shooting, killing an older man who served as a guard to the Judenrat. The two partisans escaped through the window in the chaos. No one knows how the Gestapo chief arrived at the same time as the two partisans. Was he tipped off?

The Gestapo chief ordered the Judenrat to produce the two partisans by midnight. It was an impossible demand. The Judenrat did not have direct links with the partisans, and there was not enough time to send people into the forest to find them.

At 11 p.m., the Gestapo chief told the Judenrat to stop looking for the partisans and wait for another announcement before midnight. An order came from Gestapo headquarters to liquidate the ghetto over the next four days, starting in the morning. They divided the ghetto into quadrants of 2,500 people. One quadrant would be transported each day. At 6 a.m. on January 28, 1943, the transport of the first quadrant began. They allowed each person to take whatever could fit in a knapsack. Horses and wagons lined up to bring people to the train station.

That morning, some Polish guards received bribes so that two people from the ghetto could get to the forest and let the partisans there know what was happening in the Pruzhany ghetto. Preparations began to receive all the groups planning to flee and join their assigned groups in the forest. They also considered going back to the ghetto and setting fires to distract the Germans and make it easier for people to escape. They decided not to start fires, viewing that as too risky. If they failed or got caught, it would be more difficult for people to escape.

They had not completed a tunnel from inside the ghetto to the fence line. Time did not allow for the final preparation of their plan. It was now or never to escape.

The Elman family lived in the quadrant scheduled for liquidation on January 29, the second day. On January 28, Shmeryl, now twenty-three, and Yossel, twenty, said goodbye to their family. Their sister Chaika, age seventeen, begged them to take her with them. She wanted to join the partisans and not go to the death camps. Their answer was no, as the brothers honored their agreement that no women could join them. They left their family and walked to their underground bunker to prepare for their next steps.

I cannot imagine the conflict and pain Shmeryl and Yossel shouldered during these moments of saying goodbye to their mother, sisters, aunts, and grandparents under these circumstances. Their father had recently committed suicide, and now they were leaving their mother and sisters. They would never see each other again. It is gut-wrenching.

The reality for all Jews who chose to flee was that any decision they made meant death to others no matter what they did. Had they taken Chaika with them, she could have been killed. Then they would have wondered if she would have survived going to the death camp as others did. There was no decision possible for any Jews without lingering guilt or regret. The only conclusion to avoid pain, suffering, guilt, and remorse was death—the decision Binyamin made.

After leaving their family, Shmeryl and Yossel joined the others in a barn near the ghetto fence that evening, preparing for their escape. When they got to the barn, they discovered one group member brought his wife and sister, and another had brought his wife.

The Elman brothers were furious that the women were there because they had kept their word and honored the agreement by not bringing their sister Chaika. They thought about going back and getting Chaika, but there was no time, and it would be too dangerous for the entire group to wait. Shmeryl and Yossel talked about their feelings of guilt for leaving Chaika behind their entire lives. They both said they were sure she would have survived with them.

The group of twenty left the barn and approached the ghetto fence. Two in the group ran ahead to the fence to cut the wires. German guards discovered them and started shooting. One of them fell to the ground; the other ran back, injured. Yossel Elman ran to help the one down and pulled him several hundred meters back. He died in Yossel's arms. The group retreated to the barn in defeat and then hid underground again.

The group of now eighteen made a second attempt the night of January 29. They saw the German guards with their spotlights and decided it was too risky. They decided to make another try the following evening. They agreed there would be no retreat on this attempt. They would either successfully escape or die.

On the evening of January 30, they left their bunkers and headed to the barn, carrying seven rifles, two machine guns, twelve grenades, and minimal supplies. The Germans had liquidated three-quarters of the ghetto by that day, and there were fewer guards. When they got to the barn, they discovered a large group of people in the streets near the barn. They were men, women, and children who gathered to find organized youths fleeing. They intended to follow them out. Others had done the same with earlier groups who fled.

These other people had no weapons, supplies, or even white linen to cover themselves. The presence of these people worried the group of eighteen. A large group of people would catch the guards' attention, but it was now or never. Two in the organized group ran to the fence, quickly cut the wires, and slid under the cut wires on their bellies in the snow. The white linen was good camouflage in the deep snow. The rest of the organized group followed right behind them. Shmeryl was the last to get through the fence. He saw the other large group following him. The Germans detected them and started shooting, but somehow, the entire group of eighteen made it through unharmed. Many of the other people who followed were killed, injured, or captured by guards. Overall, about forty people from this other group made it through the fence unharmed.

On January 31, 1943, the Germans completed the liquidation. The Pruzhany ghetto and the long history of its Jews no longer existed.

There were many Jews who remained hiding inside the ghetto. They had built bunkers in the basements of their homes and hid in them. About 2,000 people hid in these bunkers. Most planned to stay in their bunkers for days, even weeks, and would try to escape after the Germans were no longer guarding the ghetto. Most of these people got caught and did not survive.

The Elman brothers did not know that Moishe Yudevitsh and his wife, Rivche (Kaplan) Yudevitsh, hid in the ghetto. Rivche was the Elman brothers' cousin. Her father was Chaim Kaplan, brother of Shmeryl and Yossel Elman's mother, Seryl (Kaplan) Elman. Moishe had previously built a bunker inside a stable next to their shared house with Rivche's family.

Months before that, a friend of Moishe invited him to join the groups of young people, like the Elman brothers, to flee into the forests and join the partisans. Moishe declined because he could not take his wife, Rivche, with him. He instead developed a plan for both to hide and escape on their own.

However, they could not include their four-year-old daughter, Tsveeyah. She was too young to remain silent in the bunker. She would not survive living in what could be weeks or months in the bitterly freezing weather once they escaped.

As they debated this dilemma, their parents, sisters, and brothers convinced them they had to hide in the bunker and escape. The family also convinced them to leave Tsveeyah with both grandmothers. In either situation, Tsveeyah likely would not survive. She could live her last days with the rest of the family in the care of her grandmothers. Perhaps they would all somehow survive and be together again. For Moishe and Rivche, this was a heartbreaking decision.

The German schedule had transport for the family listed for January 31. At 3 a.m., Rivche's parents, Tsveeyah, and most other family members walked with Moishe and Rivche to their bunker. When they arrived, Moishe and Rivche hugged and kissed Tsveeyah and the rest of the family goodbye. It was a heartbreaking moment.

They climbed into the bunker. Rivche's father, Chaim, then covered the opening of the bunker with boards, dirt, and garbage. He did his best to prevent the bunker from detection by German soldiers who would later go house to house looking for Jews in hiding. At 7 a.m., the family walked to the transports. They were part of the final 2,500 Jews evacuated from Pruzhany. They would never see each other again.

Later that day, the Germans came and searched the stable. They did not detect the well-hidden bunker.

Pruzhany ghetto liquidation

9

JOURNEY IN THE FOREST

The Elman brothers and the others who got through the ghetto fence ran as quickly as possible in the heavy snow toward the forest. Two of the eighteen, the Siegal brothers, knew where they were to meet up with the ten Jewish partisans who were already in the woods. They expected to connect with the other group that night. They carried only their weapons, and only one brought food because all their provisions were with the other group in the forest. The snow was thick, and it was bitterly cold. When they arrived at the agreed-upon location, no one was there. Were they stood up, or did the other group decide it was too risky to come there?

They quickly realized that while they had planned for the escape, they knew nothing about living and surviving in the forest. The group they were meeting up with was going to train them. But now, they were lost and had no clue where to go. They kept walking into the woods through the night to see if they could find any other organized partisans. By morning, they had found no one.

They wandered around the forest for more than three weeks,

eating snow for water. They had no food or supplies. They were cold and wet.

After three weeks of wandering, they realized they had to stop searching for the other group, get organized, and begin fending for themselves. Their priority was obtaining food. They saw a small farm, surrounded the farmer with their weapons, and took food and supplies. As they were leaving, the farmer started running away, most likely to tell the Germans they were there. They had no choice but to shoot the farmer. With that, they had committed their very first act of killing someone.

They moved on and picked a location to set up a base. The group built four bunkers separated from one another. They did this so they would not be too close to each other for safety but close enough to remain in close contact. They slept in their new bunkers that night. In the morning, they came out of their bunkers and saw a local Polish forester, who also saw them. They had to kill him. The forester would turn them in if they did not. They continued to learn the cruel art of survival as partisans on their own.

Deciding they needed to gather food on a larger scale the next day, they walked to another farm and stole food items. They did not encounter anyone at the farm. They believed no one had detected them, and they returned to their bunkers. That night, they again slept in their bunkers.

Shmeryl Elman woke up in the early morning. He took his boots off before he went to sleep because they were soaking wet from wading through a swamp the previous day. In the morning, they were still wet. He decided he would start a campfire above ground to dry them off. They also needed the fire to cook breakfast. He got out of the bunker in his bare feet to gather wood piled nearby and start the fire. He took his rifle because one rule was to never be out of a bunker without your weapon. As he walked to grab some pieces of firewood, he saw a small group of German soldiers approaching from the distance. The Germans had detected their footprints in the snow and followed them toward the bunkers. They were most likely there because someone saw them at the farm the previous day and alerted the Germans.

Everyone else was still in the bunkers. Shmeryl fired off two warning shots to get the attention of the others. The Germans started shooting. The others in the bunkers heard the shooting and got out. Those in the bunker furthest away heard nothing. They did not get out. Those who heard the warning ran as fast as they could, Shmeryl still in his bare feet. The Germans threw grenades into the bunker, killing nine people. One teenage girl survived but was injured and taken. They most probably killed her. The rest of the group returned later and saw what remained. They buried their nine friends, packed up what they could, and decided they needed to move deeper into the forest. One of those killed was the brother of Yitzhak Frydberg, one of the original organizers of the Pruzhany partisans. Yitzhak fled with a different group and survived.

They moved through the forest and then separated into four groups, deciding that staying together was not safe. They needed to go their separate ways to survive and find other partisan groups. Each group would become autonomous, not knowing where the others went. In total, they had seven rifles. They split up the rifles and then went their separate ways. Shmeryl and Yossel's group took two rifles.

Meanwhile, on February 17, 1943, Moishe and Rivche (the Elmans' cousin) left the bunker in Pruzhany and traveled to a village where they knew Christians they could trust. The Christians hid them until March 10. They then left for the forest and connected with Russian partisans. They joined with them to fight the Germans and seek revenge. They were the only two from Pruzhany with that partisan group.

After the four groups split up in the forest, Shmeryl and Yossel's group of eight continued through the woods. Soon, they needed food again. Shmeryl, Yossel, and a third person walked together to find food. While they were out, they saw a horse and wagon coming toward them on the road, going through the forest. Without detection, they stayed hidden behind trees and got close enough to hear what the two people in the wagon were saying. They listened to the two speaking Russian and knew they had to be Russian partisans. They approached the wagon, and the wagon stopped. They explained to the two Russians who they were and their predicament.

The two in the wagon told them they were Belarus White Russians from a partisan unit in the forest nearby. Shmeryl, Yossel, and the third person asked if their group could join them. In their minds, they felt they had no other choice, given their current situation. Associating with White Russians was risky for Jews. White Russians were antisemitic and known for killing Jewish partisans.

The two White Russians responded that it was not their decision. They needed to talk with their commander. They agreed to speak with their commander and then return to an agreed-upon location.

They returned a few days later, telling the Jewish men they could not join their group. Everyone did not have a rifle and having Jews in their group would put them at risk because the Germans were looking for Jews. They told the Jews they had to leave that area. Every partisan group controlled its region. Partisans could not operate in areas controlled by other partisans. The White Russians said they would take them to a new place to establish themselves independently.

The Belarus White Russians took them to a forest near Yenin, where the Germans previously chased their group out. There were existing bunkers and a camp there that they could use. They found food left behind. The White Russians also told them to stay in this area and never return to where they had just left. If they returned, they would kill them. Later, the Jews figured out the real motive for bringing them to this new area. They were set up to be killed by German patrols.

Much later, they found out that this White Russian partisan group had randomly met the original Jewish group they planned to meet up with when they escaped the ghetto. They were the group that never showed up. The White Russians killed seven of the ten in that group. That is why they did not show up.

After some time in this new location, they saw smoke in the distance. The group walked to investigate the source of the smoke and came upon a group of Jewish partisans from another village near Pruzhany. Yossef Mazritskey led this Jewish partisan group. It was a family camp that included women and children. The men fought as partisans, supplying food, shelter, supplies, and protection for the women and children. The women would cook, wash clothes, and take care of the children. The children performed chores inside the camp.

After talking for a while, the two groups agreed to combine. They stayed several hundred yards apart with their bunkers. They went out together for food, supplies, and protection.

Shmeryl, Yossel, and several others walked along the main road looking for food one night. Meeting a group of Russian partisans, they shared their story and circumstances and asked to join the Russians. The Russians said they would have to talk with their commander. They agreed on a place to meet a few days later.

As agreed, the Russians returned with their commander, PA Novikov. Novikov would become a highly regarded Russian commander of the Kalinin Brigade. He wanted to meet with them. Novikov made it clear to the Jewish group that they violated the partisan code. First, they had robbed and killed ordinary peasants and farmers for food, weapons, and supplies. What they had done was unacceptable behavior for the partisans. He pointed out that these peasants and farmers were not enemies. They, too, were trying to survive. The enemy was the Germans and their local collaborators. Those were the people they should attack for weapons, food, and supplies. Second, everyone in the group did not have a gun, had no training, and lacked experience attacking Germans and sabotaging their operations. For those reasons, they could not join their partisan unit.

However, he also told them he wanted to train and prepare them. They had the potential to be good partisan fighters.

Novikov liked having Jews in his unit because he recognized how fiercely they fought when trained. They did not fear death. Revenge created the fiercest of all fighters. He committed to assigning five people from his unit to the Jewish group to train and prepare them. They would have to prove they were worthy. Then, they could join the Russian Kalinin Brigade.

First, they were trained in sabotaging telephone lines and train tracks. Next was blowing up trains and then attacking Germans by surprise, killing them and taking their weapons, ammunition, food, supplies, and uniforms.

They performed missions that included going back to Pruzhany to blow up the headquarters of the Gestapo and seize supplies. They also went on missions to cut down telephone poles to disable German telephone and telegraph communications.

Later, they were on a mission to attack Germans inside a local White Russian farmer's house. Germans regularly came to this house to have sex with attractive local women brought there for their pleasure. The Germans had an ongoing arrangement with the farmer. They forced him to do this for his family's and the women's lives. The partisans in training attacked the house and killed the Germans, confiscating twelve rifles, ammunition, food, supplies, and clothing. Shmeryl took a German uniform, which he wore for the rest of his time as a partisan. They left the farmer, his family, and the women unharmed.

After months of training, they completed missions successfully and joined the Kalinin Brigade.

On May 1, 1943, Stalin consolidated all partisan groups and established a central command. Hundreds of partisans became the Kirov combat brigade, including about seventy Jews. The brigade consisted of four smaller groups. They assigned Shmeryl and Yossel to separate groups. Many missions involved multiple groups, so Shmeryl and Yossel fought together many times. The Kirov Brigade operated in the heavily forested area near Brest and Minsk's central railroad line. Their focus was on a section of the line between Pruzhany and Ruzena.

As the Russian command became more organized, they set up

communications and planning with the Russian military. The Russian army began dropping supplies from airplanes using parachutes. Later, partisan groups built and protected landing strips in the forests so Russian planes could land and take off for more significant supply deliveries.

They attacked German patrols, supply trains and cut power and communication lines. They mined roads and bridges, disrupting the movement of troops, equipment, and supplies to the main front with Russia.

Kolka Mariak was in command of the second group, where Yossel was a member. This commander had developed a liking for Yossel and gave him more responsibility.

Yossel told Mariak about the Lehman Bandits and their atrocities in Pruzhany. They were the group of Germans with the dogs who randomly attacked and killed Jews, including the Elman brothers' uncle. The commander never forgot what Yossel told him. He gave these Jewish partisans from Pruzhany an opportunity for revenge while also performing a critical mission to sabotage German telephone and telegram communications. Several other groups took part in this mission, including Shmeryl's. The Jewish partisans in the Kirov Brigade would fight their fiercest battle ever.

Shmeryl Elman's diary contains a specific record of the battle with Lehman's Bandits:

June 1943:

The second group made two lines. It's already midday. The commander of the second group, named Mariak, told everyone to be ready for the night's departure. Those who feel sick must say so. Lines break up, and everyone takes care of tasks such as cleaning guns and other needs. No one knows what it's all about. We just know they arranged the confrontation with the enemy. As soon as the sun goes down, we start our way. We were about eighty men. We carried bags and hatchets.

We were heading to the Pruzhany-Ruzshinoi route. We walked fast but calmly because we had to cross over the border of White Russia and Eastern Prussia. At night, we reached our destination.

They split us into groups and ordered us to cut down the telephone poles, pull the cables, and then meet at a fixed place. We didn't linger, and all the telephone poles through 4 km got cut down on the route. The communication between both cities was interrupted. The commander told us we would stay there until the dawn to "welcome" the Lehman murderers that would surely come to fix the telephones and telegraphs. The task was clear. We were to get our revenge against the brutal Lehman murderers who brutalized and killed so many Jews, including my uncle.

We took position along the route along 1/2 km. We had to wait three hours until dawn, and we all lay down to sleep, except the guards.

The commander asked us to remain calm and said we'd wait for the enemy once we woke up at dawn. The night was over. As soon as the sun rose, we were all alert, waiting for the enemy. About 9 a.m., two trucks appear in the distance, driven by Germans. We made our last preparations, and we took our fight positions.

The first truck moved forward, and when it was 30 meters away, the commander ordered: fire! Organized in two lines, we open fire on the Germans, and the result is splendid. The truck was set on fire, and only one man survived, disappearing on the thistles with no hat or guns.

The second truck stopped, taking defensive positions on the other side of the route, starting a dense fire. The fight reached its maximum point. The commander ordered the right-wing to attack, and we threw ourselves at the enemy. The combat was hand-to-hand. They defended themselves strongly, but we destroyed them quickly. I hurled myself at a fat German, whom I hurt. I got on him. He had a gun in his hand, and he was trying to hurt me, but he couldn't do it because my hands thrust on his greasy neck, and I choked him to death.

There were some deceased and injured on our side. The number is unknown to us. We had the following picture before us: six Germans lying on the route, some alive, which we exterminated later. Both trucks were burning. Some people took the Germans' boots off, and others took more stuff. Others collected the guns. I'm glad to have the fat German's gun. I walk calmly between the wounded Germans. One of them says to me in Polish, he's got a wife and three children, but that doesn't soften my heart for this Lehman Bandit. A bullet in his head makes him silent.

I am amazed by myself. I could not destroy a human creature, and now

I have become a savage and have no mercy for a human being. I know the reason. These are not humans. They are Germans worse than beasts. They hurt my family members. I don't feel compassion for them. I feel satisfaction when I see their blood spreading.

The fight is over. All the German Lehman murderers are dead. We divide into two groups. One picks up our deceased and injured, and then we go back to the camp. The other group I belong to was directed to lay mines on the route and set the wooden bridge on fire.

Shortly afterward, reinforcements came to help set mines under the thirty-five German deceased. The Germans who were coming back to collect the dead would meet their death. The first truck with Germans ran over a mine and flipped over. The other trucks blockaded our way, and we couldn't pass to the other side of the route. It was guarded by motorcycles. Three of our men tried to cross over. They failed and died. Thirty-nine of us stayed on the other side of the route. Our situation was complicated. We spread all over a spacious front, and we kept constant and strong fire with all kinds of guns.

We got to cross the route, and we lost two more men there. When reaching the camp, we heard that, besides the five deceased, we had lost another 7, and there were four wounded.

Fortunately, I found my brother in the camp, who was unhurt in the fight. On his side, a German pistol was hanging. His commander had fallen during the battle. The atmosphere at the camp was depressing, given the human loss of that day. We prepared for the burial of the deceased. The 3rd group carried out this task because our men were exhausted.

Another battle they fought started when the German army found out that a Russian plane had landed in the forest nearby to drop supplies for the partisans. They dispatched hundreds of soldiers to capture the plane. Word reached the Russian partisan command of the German plans. The command sent the Kirov partisans to defend the plane and kill the Germans. They waited in the forest for the Germans and surprised them. The aircraft remained secure, completed its supply delivery, and took off. There were heavy German casualties and small losses among the partisans.

Each partisan group had assigned zones to blow up trains. If one zone were unsuccessful, the next zone would do it. If they were unsuccessful, the next zone would do it. There were very few trains that got past the partisans this way. They constantly blew up tracks, trains, trucks, tanks, roads, bridges, ammunition depots, and other equipment. They also shot down airplanes.

They ambushed soldiers, attacked garrisons, and took weapons, ammunition, artillery, anti-tank weapons, food, and supplies. In one mission, Shmeryl's group brought back five hundred cows.

Yossel trained to become the operator of the one anti-tank weapon (PTO) that his group in the Kirov Brigade captured. The capture of this weapon now allowed them to destroy German tanks. For Yossel, this was a promotion and a significant role in the group. This assignment confirmed the commander's confidence in Yossel. He was enormously proud to have this responsibility. He destroyed German tanks using this PTO.

Still, antisemitism among non-Russian partisans was always a problem. Polish, Ukrainian, Lithuanian, and White Russian partisans would kill Jews at any opportunity. They killed thousands of Jewish partisans while simultaneously fighting the Germans.

A Ukrainian became commander of Shmeryl's group. This commander was mean to everyone and did not like Jews. In particular, he did not like Shmeryl. He told Shmeryl he would see to his death. Since the Russian command did not tolerate antisemitism in the partisans, the commander could not outright kill Shmeryl. In addition, the partisan code prohibited hurting or killing another partisan, including Jews. So, the antisemitic partisans figured out effective ways to kill Jews while still staying within the rules.

The most common tactic to kill Jewish partisans involved deliberately depriving them of sleep. Death was the punishment if a partisan fell asleep while on guard duty. All partisans had missions that involved days without sleep. If someone in leadership wanted to have a Jew killed, they would have them assigned to immediate guard duty upon return from an exhausting extended mission. Often, they were assigned to multiple consecutive shifts of guard duty. A partisan could not refuse to obey orders. That, too, was punishable by death. So, this became the ultimate setup for killing Jews by antisemitic partisans.

Jews subjected to this knew they were being set up for death, but they could do nothing about it. If they refused to obey orders, they were killed for a legitimate reason. They were also killed for a legitimate reason if they were caught falling asleep on guard duty. While on guard duty, the antisemites setting them up would watch them so they could immediately see them sleeping. They would then shoot them on the spot, most often with the victim's weapon. Many Jewish partisans died this way.

Shmeryl returned to camp from a mission where he had not slept for four nights. As soon as he returned, the commander had him assigned to immediate guard duty. He complained to the commander about not sleeping for four nights, explaining how exhausted he was. He was then told to obey orders. So, he had no choice. He went on guard duty, knowing he was being set up. Shmeryl knew he would fall asleep, so he took his rifle and wrapped the barrel with cloth around his arm. That way, if he fell asleep, it would not be easy for anyone to grab his rifle and shoot him.

He completed his guard duty without falling asleep. When he returned to the main camp, the commander assigned him to the very next shift.

Shmeryl went back on guard duty again with his rifle wrapped around his arm. This time, he fell asleep. The Ukrainian commander came up to him and tried to grab his rifle to shoot him. Since Shmeryl had wrapped the barrel around his arm, the commander could not grasp it, and in trying, Shmeryl woke up. He wrestled with the commander and prevented him from taking his rifle away. The commander then started shouting at him, telling him he had fallen asleep and would be taken back to camp to be shot. Shmeryl said he did not fall asleep and told the commander to prove it.

Two other Russian guards were on duty with Shmeryl, and

they had observed everything. They disliked the commander and told him that Shmeryl did not fall asleep. The commander got angry and shouted, "All three of you fell asleep." That meant he intended to have all three of them shot to death.

Shmeryl raised his rifle and shot the commander dead with two shots. The three of them then rushed to move his body away from them and laid him on the ground to make it appear that Shmeryl shot him from a distance. They knew the shots got the attention of everyone back at the camp, and others would soon be on their way to see what happened.

Another commander and a few others ran to the scene. This commander asked what was going on. Shmeryl responded that the three of them were on guard. They heard the noise of someone approaching them and asked them to stop and say the secret code. Shmeryl continued that there was no response, so he asked two more times, and there was still no response. Since it was dark, he could not see who it was, so he shot the intruder. (In the partisans, a daily code word had to be used when asked for identity by guards. If you did not say the code word, it meant you did not belong there, and the guards could legitimately shoot.) The two other guards corroborated Shmeryl's story. That closed the case on what happened.

Shmeryl and the other two men who had been on guard duty with him continued in their assigned roles and missions with the group. But at the same time, the new commander and others continued to wonder what happened in the shooting incident. Shmeryl knew there were suspicions, but he felt comfortable that the truth would never be uncovered. Shmeryl not only saved his own life, but he also saved the lives of many other Jewish partisans. Using the falling asleep trap, the Ukrainian commander would have continued setting up Jewish partisans for death.

SHMERYL LEAVES THE KIROV
BRIGADE

A few weeks after Shmeryl killed the Ukrainian commander, in early 1944, the Russian military dropped a group of fifty Russian paratroopers to set up a partisan presence in the Bialowieza Forest. This forest is seventy kilometers from Pruzhany. They had dropped the Russian paratroopers to connect with the Kirov partisan group for this effort.

The Bialowieza Forest was one of the most extensive forests in the region and a well-known hunting area. Gestapo founder Hermann Goring would regularly hunt in this forest after the German occupation of Poland.

The German army occupied all the villages in this forest to prevent the partisans from entering. This forest area was very strategic to the Germans because it straddled Poland and Belarus. To the Russians, it was essential to push the Germans out and have the Russian partisans control the forest.

The paratroopers asked for partisans who knew the villages, roads, and forest area to guide them. The new commander, still suspicious of the circumstances associated with the shooting of the Ukrainian commander, wanted Shmeryl and the two other men out of his unit. This request presented the opportunity to move them to a dangerous mission with the paratroopers. The three were assigned to these paratroopers as their guides. Shmeryl and Yossel would now be separated for the first time.

The commander of the paratroopers was Russian, and Shmeryl developed an excellent relationship with him. Shmeryl knew the area well and took them to the Bialowieza Forest. They had to bypass all the villages occupied by the Germans and wade through the swamps. Before entering the forest, they needed to gather food and supplies.

They stopped near a small town and set up camp. Shmeryl and the other two partisans scouted the area to see what they would face if they attacked. They saw about 150 Ukrainians occupying the town for the Germans.

That night, the entire group surrounded and attacked the Ukrainians by surprise and took control of the town. They then took around fifty horses and wagons filled with hogs, cattle, other food, and supplies and traveled back to the camp they had set up.

Shmeryl recommended they leave and head into the deep forest for cover, which the partisans always did after a raid. The camp was out in the open and easily detected. Since it was night, the paratrooper commander decided they would sleep there and move into the forest in the morning.

Later that night, German planes and soldiers attacked them. They fled the camp and ran into the forest. Twenty of the fifty paratroopers were killed. Shmeryl and the two other partisans were unharmed. As they fled into the woods, the Germans feared following them, not knowing if more partisan reinforcements would attack. The Germans always feared the forest, believing there could be a partisan behind every tree.

The paratrooper commander decided they were too small of a group to take on the well-established Germans in the Bialowieza Forest. He wanted to do more scouting of the entire forest area to figure out the exact scope of what they faced and then share the information with the Russian partisan command. He split them into four separate groups to scout different areas. They would then meet six weeks later at this exact location in the forest.

Shmeryl was the group leader. They were assigned to go near Bialystok. After about a week, they approached a small town and saw smoke in a distant forest area. They went toward the smoke to see what was there. They found a small camp that had six people. They were Russian prisoners of war who escaped from a German prisoner-of-war camp. One was a Jewish doctor. They had all been wounded escaping, and they had hidden in the forest to survive. The doctor had treated them for their wounds. The Russians asked Shmeryl to let them join their group.

Shmeryl had no hesitation because most partisan groups did not have doctors. Medical care for the wounded was impossible to provide. If an injured partisan could not travel to the next place, they had to be shot so as not to burden the rest of the group or be left behind and then caught and tortured by the Germans. All would welcome a doctor in their group. The five other trained Russian soldiers would be an asset to the partisans. They wanted to fight.

The six Russians traveled with Shmeryl's group for the remaining five weeks as they scouted their assigned area. They then traveled back to the original meeting point from which they had started. The paratrooper commander and the rest of the group praised Shmeryl and his group for finding and bringing a doctor to them, along with five soldiers.

The larger group traveled together for about two more weeks within that forest area. The Germans were in that entire area. They had to be careful and feared being discovered and attacked again.

They finished the scouting work, vacated the area, and worked their way back to a place called Baranovichi. They knew other large partisan groups were located there. They discovered a sizable all Jewish group of partisans, about five hundred total. These partisans came from several small towns.

There was another Jewish group that had over 1,000 people in it, including women and children. This group had prepared ahead of the liquidation of their towns and escaped in large numbers. It was a family camp like the Bielskis,' one of the most famous and written about partisan groups.

They continued to Baranovichi, where they connected with and joined a brigade under Russian Major-General PP Kapusta. General Kapusta previously commanded the Russian troops with Sokoly as his headquarters. General Kapusta now commanded about 20,000 partisans in the Bialystok area. The German army itself was no match for this size of partisan organization.

From 1939 to 1941, General Kapusta led his battalion of Russian soldiers. In 1941, when the Germans invaded Russia, they surrounded General Kapusta's battalion as they retreated from the Sokoly/Bialystok area. The German forces captured many, including the general. His leg was injured in that battle.

While in the prisoner-of-war camp, General Kapusta was determined to escape and form a partisan group to fight the Germans. There were fourteen other members of his Russian army group in the POW camp that he trusted and confided in. In spring 1942, they developed a plan to escape from the POW camp. Over time, they dug an opening under the fence that would allow them to crawl through and run. The opening was undetected.

One night, they saw the right opportunity, ran to that opening, and slid under the fence. They were detected after most got through, and German guards began shooting from the guard tower. They all escaped to the forest. Like all new partisan groups, they had to obtain weapons, food, and supplies. Two in the group were White Russians who knew the area well. A third person was Jewish. Local peasants who disliked the Germans helped them obtain arms, food, and supplies. Over a brief period, they connected with Jewish partisans in the forest who joined them. The group grew to over 140 people, most of whom were Jews. They continued to grow as they encountered Soviet soldiers caught behind enemy lines in the forest who joined them. They became one of the largest Russian partisan groups in eastern Belarus, known as the "Kapusta Gang." They wreaked havoc on the Germans.

In December 1942, Hitler's deputy in Belarus mobilized German forces and police to attack and annihilate the Kapusta Gang. The Kapusta Gang won that battle with heavy German casualties and only a few on their end. After that, the Germans avoided any fighting with the Kapusta Gang.

Stalin's chain of command, recognizing the leadership of General Kapusta, reassigned him to build up an equivalent partisan presence in the Bialystok region, including the Bialowieza Forest. They took over the west side of the forest. Shmeryl Elman's paratrooper group was operating from the far east side, still controlled by the Germans. Their retreat to the west of the forest brought them into General Kapusta's area.

The Kapusta partisan battalion was large and eventually controlled most of that area. They set up the towns they now held as headquarters for the different brigades, just like the main army. They occupied this area way ahead of the Russian military. Shmeryl and his group became brigade members that held a triangular region between the Chara and Nieman Rivers. The Germans still controlled the forest on the other side of the Nieman River on the east.

When they went on missions for food and supplies, they used three primitive wood pontoon boats they built to cross the river and set up a beachhead. They would march through a series of German-controlled villages, round up as much as five hundred head of cattle, and lead the herd back to the river and over the pontoon boat bridgehead.

The Russian POW doctor in Shmeryl's old group established a field hospital for the Kapusta partisans in that area. Shmeryl joined many missions to get medical supplies and medicines from the various villages. This field hospital saved the lives of hundreds of partisans.

While the Germans controlled the entire forest on the other side of the river, they never attempted an attack. The partisans in numbers, weapons, and equipment were equal to the Germans, but they were superior. The Germans feared any engagement with them.

Shmeryl Elman's brigade later focused on disrupting the German supply chain. They were assigned to daily missions to blow up all German transportation and communication modes. Shmeryl paired up with the machine gun operators. His job was to supply the ammunition belts to the machine gun and keep the ammunition flowing into the machine gun during battles. The machine gunners would set up around the perimeter where something would be blown up. While others put down the dynamite, mines, and fuses, they would protect the entire group from any attacks.

He also scouted for Germans on some of these missions. Each scout had a pistol with a silencer. They would sneak up on them and shoot them when they encountered Germans. The silencers prevented other German soldiers from hearing anything. If Germans got past the pistol-carrying scouts, the machine gunners would get them. Often, the Germans fled when they heard the gunfire.

When the partisans blew up a train, they had to record the number of the boxcar, the location, and the contents. They then transmitted this information to Moscow. In Moscow, they tracked the data to record German losses. They would also broadcast information about these attacks over the radio to bolster the spirit of the Russian people and troops. The Kapusta battalion had a group of three women who only worked on communications with Moscow. They used transmitters and receivers powered by crank-driven generators to send and receive communications from Moscow.

In the spring of 1944, it was becoming clear the end of the war was near. The Russian air force controlled the skies. All German troops and their supply chain fled the Russian front as fast as possible. The Germans were living in chaos and fear. Their strict sense of organization and control when they invaded Russia was destroyed.

The battles between German and Russian troops got closer and closer. As the Russians pushed retreating Germans back, the partisans would attack them from the rear. They continued to blow up the transportation and communications assets of the Germans. The Germans abandoned their equipment and supplies as they fled through the forests to avoid the partisans. The partisans controlled the main roads and towns they had to travel through.

The Germans were sandwiched between the Russian army and the partisans. The partisans occupied cities and towns, marching from the east while the Russians marched west. The Germans suffered heavy casualties during their retreat. At some point, the Russian command ordered the partisans to take prisoners rather than continue the onslaught of the retreating Germans. They took tens of thousands of Germans to POW camps that were built.

Shmeryl's brigade occupied the city of Vawkavysk before the Russian army did. Yossel was in Russian-occupied Pruzhany at the same time. However, neither knew the status of the other. The last time they saw each other was when Shmeryl left the Kirov Brigade.

The following are Shmeryl Elman's diary entries while serving under General Kapusta.

January 5, 1944

We left the village "Moskaly," and we met at a farm. The situation was tense. The enemy had concentrated many military forces in our districts. They were getting ready for war actions, isolated, surprising, and fast. We were alert.

Each Chief of Partisan Commandos joined his men, returning from some action. There would not be any more groups sent for operations. The guard positions were reinforced.

Life resumed as usual. We made some food. In case of an attack from the enemy, the commander decided we would throw ourselves into an open fight since we were not out of war supplies.

Ten men, including myself, were on the defense points. Our duty was to patrol along the village Moskaly at the lake. There was joy in our area. At night, people would dance and play. I decided to dance too. This new attitude made my friends think about a situation that would change their destiny soon.

April 22, 1944

A large number of Germans have arrived in "Korilivich" and "Malkovich." The same happened in Krupitzky. We were hoping one of these days, the blockade would begin. In the camp, we put all the foodstuffs from the stores underground. There was serenity in general. The newcomer partisans were afraid to die, and we promised they would get used to things in time. Our life was going on normally. The patrol would search the area, and many times spies infiltrated. Unfortunately, we could not hurt them. We could only report them to the superior command.

I often take a bath in the pond because the "pritzn" began to show again (the way we call the lice). They are worse than Germans. It amazed us to see the way they appeared again. The situation we were living under was to blame. In the evening, a German plane used to fly over our area.

April 23, 1944

The Nieman River was also blockaded. Many Cossacks turned up in the villages. Our positions in the eastern area were reinforced. We dug trenches in the Krupitzky area since the enemy could attack from that side. The peasants were nervous and aggressive. They were moving all their belongings into the forest as well. Each man takes his position for defense. Borders are demarcated. The enemy lies in wait for us all around.

April 24, 1944

While we were sleeping, the guard woke us up because artillery and mines were coming from Sokoly, on the Nieman River. This was a tactic of the enemy before the attack. We deduced they could attack from the Nieman side. There was calm among us. The gunshots continued, and it was getting stronger. The air was wrapped in shadows because of the explosions. Little by little, we heard the partisan gunshots. That meant they went to face the enemy. Many of the boats they were sailing in sank with their men. Others went back, leaving dead and drowned men. At midday, the calm returned.

April 29, 1944

May 1st is getting closer. We made the last preparations for the celebration. It was a lunch with alcoholic drinks for every partisan. After breakfast, they sent me with six men to collect firewood for the kitchen for two days while the celebration would last. They ordered us to keep guard near the lake when we returned at lunchtime because the enemy may unexpectedly attack May 1st. That news annoyed us pretty much, for we wouldn't be able to be at the May 1st celebrations. But, with patience, we had to do our duty. Each one of us picked his belongings and got ready to walk. At night, we reached the village Moskaly beside the lake, and we took the guard. There we knew there was loads of meat, and we decided to change meat for alcoholic drinks, for the celebration.

May 1, 1944

From early morning, drunks began to turn up in Moskaly. Our brigade's commander scolded us and warned the enemy could attack at any moment, so we should be ready, and only at night would we get our alcohol portion.

Two artillery pieces were placed in the bunkers, and we received instructions on how to fire against the enemy. One of the previous nights, we were supplied war supplies from planes, so we had enough. The movements over the lake were controlled so that spies wouldn't infiltrate our area. The boats were filled because many groups were returning from a mission, and they hurried to reach the camp and be part of the May 1st celebrations.

The day passed peacefully except for some drunk partisans who killed a peasant. At night we celebrated with a dinner, a musician was brought in, and the youth danced.

May 2, 1944

The day was peaceful. Each one of us had to take guard duty for four hours a night and four days. In my free time, I read a book I had found by chance. I tried to avoid talking to the village peasants because they were antisemitic. They were witnesses to the atrocities committed by the Nazis against Jews. I used to rage and shame them when people talked badly about Jews, for they say take the youth to death like lambs. This tortures me.

May 3, 1944

In general, there was peace. We live quite well in Moskaly. We don't feel as free as here in the countryside because there's much more space there, but we have to be always on guard. The movement on the lake doesn't stop. They sent several groups to carry out duties, and they returned after having achieved it.

The duty was to bring some food. In a word, Moskaly is a station with a partisan port by the lake's bank. We're not out of drink to make a toast, but the important thing is the exchange. Each peasant had his little wine factory, and that was his supply. We had to pay a lot for one bottle, but we partisans didn't care.

Today we live, tomorrow who knows. That's why we don't trade; we just wanted the alcohol bottle. More than once, the Germans got in, and they wanted to take revenge on people. They thought people were helping the partisans, but they couldn't do so because they were repelled, and many drowned in the lake, patrolled and controlled day and night.

Each commander had his port and village, which they considered his capital city. In an enemy attack, they left the bunkers, received the enemy with fire, and pushed them back, leaving many victims. The enemy had to join many forces to infiltrate into the partisan area, which wasn't always helpful. The Moskaly and other villages' inhabitants used to see the Germans once a year when they made raids against the partisans. They turned up with ten men, and when the war supplies began to be scarce, they left the area and went to other places. The partisans didn't have problems with the war supplies, and we could face an open fight with the enemy and then hide. The Russians dropped the war supplies and weapons with new systems from planes in parachutes.

Every night, the youth of Moskaly meet at a big house to dance and play. Then we would forget about the challenging moments we were passing through, and we left ourselves to be taken away. I don't participate in those parties, even if I have free time, because my heart is grieving for my beloved people, for they didn't have the same destiny as those dancing.

To my mind comes my brother, whom I said goodbye to during the fight against the Germans. Is he still alive? Or maybe he fell into the battle? I don't know, and he doesn't know about me. We're joined through a feeling of revenge. My home city comes up too, our desertion of my dear mother and sisters in such a terrible moment for them, when they were on the Nazi killer's hand, which annihilated them most chillingly. The view of my father hanging who ended his life for him not to see the damage done to his beloved people. All this makes me forget the hardships I had to endure during the fight against the enemy, and I demand revenge! Revenge! For the innocent blood spread, for all, I can take revenge for so much harm and horror.

May 4, 1944

Calm days. I'm not used to a life like this. The day is too long for me. In my spare time, I amuse myself by thinking about my partisan life, which is a calmed life after all. We have good food, and we do nothing, only eight hours of guard duty, and the remaining time passes slowly. The Christian friends feel good, and they try to have a good time. They want to pull me with them, but who can dance when the body doesn't want to! The peasant woman, she's very kind since I'm staying at her house. She goes all around me and doesn't know what to do for me. I know why that is. She saw what they did to others who, like me, have a Jewish name, and she felt compassion. She frequently tells me she had some Jewish friends, which she got along with, many youths like me that couldn't be saved. I never have an answer for her; I finally leave the house. There were few Christians like this, and I'm happy to have been with them. Her family comprised a husband, a son, and a daughter around 18 or 20 years old.

May 5, 1944

The sentry wakes us up. We can hear gunshots and mine explosions on the other side of the lake. We sent one of our men to the camp to transmit the news.

People are getting ready to have breakfast because the house's owner and her family have escaped to the woods for fear. We got into the trenches, and we waited to receive the enemy. They don't turn up. In the distance, we can see flames and smoke. This is a sign of the enemy setting the village on fire. All the peasants have gotten away to the nearby woods. The enemy has come. They're few. 300 men is not a big deal for us. Our commandant has moved a few kilometers on the right side of the village, Pehstzanka, just behind the enemy. We receive an order to fire to make the enemy withdraw. The Germans did their work. They set the village on fire and later left a rear guard. The others withdrew. After a one-hour truce, the partisans suddenly attacked them with a fire hurricane of all sorts of guns. Seeing they cannot defend themselves, they get away in panic, leaving their ammunition and other spoils and a bunch of deceased and injured behind. We take the ammunition, and we take all the Germans' clothing and guns. We return, having not lost one single man.

The peasants recovered their goods, but they had no housing. Now they're the forest citizens. Little by little, the peasants of Moskaly come back much more calmed to their houses in the woods. At night, the youth have fun again.

May 6, 1944

Calm days again. Lately, we're inactive; returning to the camp makes us nervous. The landlady tells us she's out of potatoes, and she had nothing else to cook. The girl gets ready to do a "bombiaske" (raid a peasant to get supplies). I stay the night on guard, and the others leave.

May 7, 1944

It's hard to stay all night long on guard duty. The fellows returned and brought alcoholic drinks, but this won't keep me warm. I sleep all day long, and I have to be on guard duty again by dawn.

May 8, 1944

The group "Politrok" that was on guard behind Slonim comes back. They have accomplished their duty. They exploded six wagons loaded with war supplies. They brought alcohol and gave us five liters. They told us the enemy concentrated behind Slonim, probably to fight against the partisans. We don't care about it because we get some drinks while we wait for the enemy.

May 9, 1944

As soon as we finish breakfast, the group "Politrok" says they will take the guard, and we return to the camp. We're happy about it because we still have to face a challenging task. We wait until midday, and at night we go back to the camp. We get ready and receive the following order: KASHIN will be the next commander of the group. The group direction was unknown. We prepare two mines of 15 kg each.

May 10, 1944

Just after breakfast, they call five of our men to receive instructions about how to operate. We're sick of always hearing the same: pay attention, drive carefully. We're annoyed, and we don't pay attention at all. We say goodbye to the other members and get ready to leave. We're heading to the lake.

When we walk the first kilometers, our shoulders feel the heavy load of the war supplies we carry. In the last weeks, we lost the habit of taking so many supplies. We walk until dusk through the area controlled by partisans, and we're heading to Slonim. At night, we lie down in Dubowka, and we have breakfast at 7 a.m.

May 11, 1944

Just after breakfast, we start walking. We have a march of twenty-four hours ahead. The march is very exhausting for us because we have rested so much at Moskaly. We leave the partisans' area in the evening, and we go unnoticed through the German area. We try to ignore them. We receive the order not to fight against them to avoid human loss. We would accomplish our duty, and we'd be back on May 20.

We rest every 3 km because we carry so much load. Rain begins to fall. Rain falls all night long, and we're soaked. The night is dark. We can't see each other, and we often have to touch the way with our hands. It's raining harder and harder, and we don't have a place to camp. If Hitler had to suffer a hundredth of the way we do, he could not take it. We envy the dogs that can burrow where they can rest. There's no burrowing for us to be in peace. Exhausted to death, soaked, and tired, we arrive in the woods behind Slonim at dawn. The rain doesn't stop. We light a fire to dry our clothes a little. We lie down very tight to warm each other up. It's raining cats and dogs, but we don't care, and we fall asleep at once. We woke up at noon. The rain stopped, and now we can think about drying ourselves. Each one makes use of his dry food since we begin to feel hungry. The next night we decided to rest because we felt exhausted and slept to death.

There are no additional diary entries available. The rest of the diary remains forever lost.

In late May 1944, the Russians occupied all of Belarus. The

Belarus partisans disbanded. The Russians then integrated the partisans into the Russian army. They did not give the partisans any choice. Both Shmeryl and Yossel now served in the Russian military.

Both brothers still did not know each other's fate. Still separated, they shared the same aspirations. They did not believe in the Russian communist system and way of life. As Jews, they also viewed life in Russia as no different from life in Poland. The Russians had a long history of antisemitism, and outside of the partisans, they understood that antisemitism remained strong. They already saw how the Russian army viewed Jews differently from the Russian partisans.

Like most other Jewish survivors, not only did they want to get the hell out of Poland and Russia, but they also saw no place for Jews in any part of Europe. Their goal was to connect with their Uncle Samuel and find their way to America. But for the time being, that was not an option for them. Refusal to serve in the Russian army resulted in death by firing squad. They did what was required and thought about how they would get out of Russia in the future.

Shmeryl's army assignment was with NKVD working out of Vawkavysk. The NKVD was the Russian secret police, the predecessor to the KGB. Shmeryl asked for an assignment in or near Pruzhany, but his request was denied.

As the Germans retreated, their Polish, Ukrainian, and Lithuanian collaborators who fought with them also retreated with them. Many of these people formed groups like partisans in the forests to attack the Russians. Shmeryl provided NKVD support to Russian army units sent into the woods to fight and flush out these groups of German collaborators. Later, he joined an NKVD group that dispatched messages to Russian authorities in the region. The NKVD operated in strict secrecy, so only sealed letters were sent via messengers like Shmeryl.

Shmeryl had an assignment to travel to Viosk, Bielsk, Bialowiez, Bialystok, and other cities to deliver a sealed letter dispatch to each

NKVD chief in those cities. This assignment took him near Pruzhany. He made a stop in Pruzhany, where he went to visit his old home. A Polish family was living in the house. He told the man who came to the door that this was his home. The man told him to go away. Shmeryl only came by to see the house, so he left. He walked around the ruins of Pruzhany and then continued his mission.

There are two things Shmeryl did not know. First, Yossel had gone to Pruzhany while he was in Vawkavysk. Yossel also visited their old home and left.

Second, Shmeryl did not know the contents of the letters he carried in the top-secret sealed envelopes. Shmeryl traveled back to Vawkavysk and later found out the letters contained the new borders between Russia and Poland. Belarus would become part of the Russian Soviet Union. The territory west, which included the cities where Shmeryl dropped off the letter, would become part of Poland. The letter also said the NKVD should begin vacating those cities to allow the Polish administration to take over.

Had Shmeryl known the contents when he was in those other cities, he would not have returned to the Russian side. He would have stayed in Bialystok, which was now inside Poland. He would have been free of the Russians. Now, he was back in Russia and had to figure out how to escape. Unknown to the Elman brothers, they were both stuck on the Russian side of the border, facing the same dilemma.

Shmeryl began planning his escape from Russia. He saw rail cars being filled with coal in Vawkavysk that left daily for cities on the Polish side of the border. He decided this would be his way out. One day, he watched the coal cars get filled for delivery to Bialystok, where he wanted to go. He climbed inside one when no one was looking and buried himself in the coal. He remained in the coal car for three days until it arrived in Bialystok. He was now free of Russian rule.

For the rest of his life, he never returned to Pruzhany for two reasons. One, he had no one to see there. Second, he knew the

Russians never forgot an army deserter, no matter how many years passed.

Through this period, the war was still underway further west. The Russians had not yet occupied Warsaw. The battles and war would not end until the fall of Berlin.

Shmeryl went to Bialystok because it was the closest large city inside the new Polish border. Most Jewish survivors that escaped Russian control in Belarus went to Bialystok for the same reason. He was also still wondering about his brother, Yossel. He hoped Yossel would also make his way to Bialystok. At the same time, Shmeryl started developing plans. He wanted to join his uncle and aunts in America.

11

YOSSEL'S JOURNEY

Yossel remained in the Kirov Brigade and assumed leadership roles. When the Russians liberated the Pruzhany region, Yossel's partisan unit was integrated into the Russian army. Yossel was named a unit commander, and his unit returned to Pruzhany to identify and capture all German collaborators. Meanwhile, Shmeryl and Yossel still had not connected and did not know if the other had survived.

Yossel stopped to visit their former home. He, like Shmeryl, spoke with the current residents and told them he used to live there. They were not happy he had come. However, the wife offered him some food. He responded that he did not need food. He was just there to see his old house. He did ask for a place to sleep for the night. He felt exhausted and had not slept for a long time. They allowed him to sleep in the house. The wife offered him breakfast in the morning, but Yossel turned her down. He knew they were short on food for their own family, and he had his food.

Soon, Yossel received word through partisan channels that Shmeryl had survived and was now in Bialystok. Shmeryl also received word that Yossel was in Pruzhany and sent him a message to come to Bialystok to be together.

Yossel spoke with his regional commander and asked to be released from the Russian army to join his only surviving brother in Bialystok. The commander rejected the request, but he offered to dispatch an airplane to Bialystok to pick up Shmeryl and bring him back to Pruzhany as an alternative. The commander may have been aware that Shmeryl was a deserter, and this plan could have been a way to capture him. Yossel would not have known that. Yossel, like Shmeryl, had no intention of remaining in Russia. Yossel turned down the offer.

The regional commander then believed Yossel would try to flee. He reassigned Yossel to another army unit inside Russia where escape would be impossible. Yossel now had to act quickly. He had to escape before he traveled to his new assignment.

Escaping was exceedingly tricky for Yossel because he was a commander and visible to his commanders and unit. He also knew they were monitoring him. Any plan to escape had a considerable risk of being detected. An attempt to escape and not succeed would also mean death.

One day in Pruzhany, Yossel ran into Dr. Olga Goldfein, walking with Sister Dolorosa in the market area. Dr. Goldfein was a neighbor of the Elman family and a highly regarded doctor in Pruzhany for Jews and Christians.

In January 1942, Sister Dolorosa (Genowefa Czubak) of the order of St. Ignatius of Loyola in Pruzhany became seriously ill. There were no Christian physicians in Pruzhany at the time. There were Jewish physicians, but they all resided inside the Jewish ghetto. The other sisters discussed what could be done and agreed that Dr. Goldfein should be sought out and brought back to treat Sister Dolorosa. The Germans allowed one of the nuns to enter the ghetto. They provided a permit to enable Dr. Goldfein to leave the ghetto to treat Sister Dolorosa. She recovered fully because of that treatment. Sister Dolorosa never forgot the kindness of Dr. Goldfein.

On January 28, 1943, Dr. Goldfein was one of the 10,000

Jews in the Pruzhany ghetto who boarded the horse and wagons and transport trains to Auschwitz. She escaped by breaking an opening into the wooden side of the train and jumping out. Dr. Goldfein was bruised up but not injured from the jump. She then walked about ten kilometers back to Pruzhany to find Sister Dolorosa at the convent, hoping she would help her.

She found Sister Dolorosa there. Dr. Goldfein received the clothing of a nun and the name Sister Helena. She stayed in the convent and lived with the nuns briefly. Soon, Mother Superior found out about Dr. Goldfein's presence and ordered both Dr. Goldfein and Sister Dolorosa to leave the convent. She was antisemitic and angry that Sister Dolorosa was helping a Jew.

Sister Dolorosa was originally from a village called Olszyny, and the two traveled there. Dr. Goldfein continued to be Sister Helena and practiced as a doctor in Olszyny under the auspices of the convent there. She treated Christians who otherwise would not have had access to a doctor.

After the Russian liberation, Dr. Goldfein and Sister Dolorosa returned to Pruzhany. Dr. Goldfein set up a place to treat Jewish survivors and Christians who needed medical attention. Sister Dolorosa returned to the convent. The Mother Superior was unhappy to see her and never forgave her for helping and rescuing a Jew. Sister Dolorosa was banished from the convent for life. She left and reassumed her given name, Genowefa Czubak. She rejoined Dr. Goldfein and assisted her with her medical work in Pruzhany. It was during this time that Yossel ran into them.

Yossel explained his situation to Dr. Goldfein and Genowefa. Dr. Goldfein also wanted to go to Bialystok to begin the effort to find out her family's status. Genowefa no longer wanted to remain in Pruzhany and would join them. They came up with a plan. They would travel in a horse-drawn wagon. Yossel would be hidden in the back of the wagon. Dr. Goldfein and Genowefa would dress as nuns and drive the wagon. Two nuns driving the wagon would lower the risk of the wagon being searched. They then left Pruzhany.

When they reached the new border between Russia and

Poland, the wagon was not searched. They crossed the border successfully and then made it to Bialystok. Shmeryl and Yossel were together again.

In Bialystok, Dr. Goldfein received word from the International Red Cross that her daughter and granddaughter were alive and lived in Nancy, France. Her son-in-law was liberated from a POW camp in Germany by the American forces. Dr. Goldfein began the long and challenging journey that took her through the displaced person camps of Austria and Germany. She reached Strasbourg in November 1945, where she was met by her daughter, who took her to her home in Nancy.

Dr. Goldfein immigrated to Israel shortly after the state was established in 1948. She resumed her medical practice there, treating many new immigrants who had survived the Holocaust in Europe and resettled in Israel. Dr. Goldfein died in 1974.

Genowefa Czubak remained in Poland, settling in the city of Lodz. She remained faithful to the church; however, she was never allowed to return as a nun. Helping a Jew was never forgiven. Yad Vashem (Israel's official memorial to victims of the Holocaust) recognized her as "Righteous Among the Nations of the World." This title was given to Christians who heroically saved the lives of Jews during the Holocaust.

12

THE POGROMS

After the Russian liberation, Jewish survivors still lived with the same risks as those under German occupation. Polish Christians still hated the Jews. Surviving Jews were attacked and killed. Several Polish Christians told the Gritczaks they were not safe staying with the Kroshevskys'. Their lives would be at risk if other Polish Christians found out they were there. They were told to go to Sokoly, where they would be safer.

The Gritczaks walked the eleven kilometers to Sokoly. Sheinche and Rochal did not have shoes and walked barefoot. It was now August and warm, much different from walking barefoot in the winter. When they arrived in Sokoly, they found ten Jews there who had returned.

They looked for Chaikovsky, the first Polish Christian who hid them when they fled. They learned the Germans arrested him years before and sent him to a work camp. No one had heard from him since. The Germans sent many other Polish Christians from Sokoly to work camps under the suspicion of helping Jews. Somehow, the Germans found out, probably because Poles turned them in.

Polish Christians had burned most of the Jewish homes in Sokoly after the ghetto was liquidated. They burned the Gritczak house. More Jews came back to Sokoly, including Shaine Olshak, the cousin of the Gritczak sisters and niece of Menucha.

Shaine was twenty-two years old. She survived in a bunker in the forest with Zeev Olshak, whom she married upon their return to Sokoly. Shaine succeeded in getting her four-year-old niece, Tulkale, back from a Christian family. Tulkale and her parents hid in the forest. During a forest search, the Germans discovered them and killed her parents. They left Tulkale alone in the woods to die. A good-hearted Christian woman found Tulkale wandering, took her home, and cared for her.

When Shaine and the other Jews returned to Sokoly, they learned that Tulkale had survived and lived with the Christian family. At first, the Christian woman was not willing to give up Tulkale. She had become attached to her. But Shaine would not give up. Finally, the Christian woman agreed to return her to her family, and Shaine took care of her with great dedication.

Zeev Gritczak arranged for an apartment for his family. He restarted his business dealings with the farmers among his Christian friends and earned a good living.

What used to be Mordechai Surasky's house became the residence of Colonel Dubroshin, the Russian commander after the Russian liberation. It was a large house with four bedrooms. On February 10, 1944, Colonel Dubroshin handed over the Surasky house to three Jewish families, numbering twelve people. One family was the Gritczaks'. The second family was Shaine and Zeev Olshak, and Tulkale. I do not know the third family.

In conducting my research, I found three sources documenting the details of the following celebration and tragedy at the Surasky house. My mother once shared a tiny part of it, but I never knew the details.

On Shabbat February 17, 1944, one-half year after their liberation, the survivors planned a celebration at the Surasky house. They would celebrate the miracle of their survival and put all the horrors they had been through behind them, at least for one night. In addition, they would celebrate a housewarming for those living in the Surasky house, the engagement of a survivor from Sokoly to a survivor from Swiccienin, and the recent return of a young man from the death camps.

Before the celebration, Sheinche visited David Zholty's mother. She was about seventy years old. David and his mother had survived together in a bunker in the forest. He was very devoted to his mother. After liberation, he was offered a job in Bialystok as an engineer. He turned the job offer down to care for his mother. Sheinche knew David's mother from before the war. She was like family. Sheinche would visit her often since returning to Sokoly. Sheinche made this visit because David and his mother would not be attending the party. The party would run late into the night—too late for David's mother.

Sheinche had to leave to get home for the celebration. It was dark out, and David offered to walk her home. David told his mother to put the tea kettle on so they could both have tea when he soon returned. He walked back with Sheinche and made a fateful decision to go inside to see everyone for a brief time before returning home.

Twenty-one people were gathered at the Surasky house. The young played cards. The elderly talked among themselves. Several women took care of the kitchen and fried latkes. David Zholty, Sheinche Gritczak, and others gathered in the kitchen to converse.

At the same time, Avrahamel Goldberg decided to seize his niece Feigele from a Polish family that had hidden her during the war and refused to return her. He arrived in Sokoly from Bialystok in a military vehicle he rented and drove to the celebration at the Surasky house. He picked up Benjamin Rachlav and Benyamin Gorkovitz, who both had pistols and volunteered to help him get Feigele. They all then left in the vehicle.

A half-hour after this group left to get Feigele, the back door of the Surasky house opened. A Pole with a large mustache, dressed in an army uniform, came in with an automatic rifle in his hand. Zeev Gritczak saw the Pole first and cried out, "Robbers have come!" He ran to the other room and locked the door.

The Pole opened a round of fire. He killed David Zholty and the soon-to-be bride from Swiccienin, Batya Weinstein, with the first shots while she fried latkes. She fell dead with a knife in her hand. A third victim was four-year-old Tulkale, Shaine Olshak's niece.

Sheinche Gritczak ran out of the house holding hands with her cousin Shaine Olshak. Other attackers were outside and fired shots at them. One bullet struck Shaine in the back and killed her. Sheinche kept running to the police station to report what was happening.

After that, the murderer entered another room full of guests and started shooting again. Panic arose. For a moment, his rifle jammed. While the murderer fixed his weapon, many celebrants broke through a window and escaped. Zeev, Menucha, Rochal, and Mina Gritczak escaped through the window.

Other Jews ran into bedrooms and hid under the beds. A kerosene lamp that stood on a table fell on the wood floor. The kerosene spread, and a small fire broke out.

More robbers entered the house and moved room by room, shooting anyone they saw. They also shot underneath the beds. Shammai Litvak was killed, and David Koschevsky was severely injured. Shammai Litvak's body covered Avraham Kalifovitz and saved him. The shots did make holes in Avraham's clothing and grazed him. A miracle saved him. Issur Wondolowicz was also killed

A thirteen-year-old boy, Sheikele Litvak, came into the house in the middle of the robbery. The murderers asked him, "To whom are you going to see?"

He answered, "My brother." (His brother was Shammai Litvak, who had been killed in the bedroom.)

One murderer shot Sheikele in the face. Sheikele covered his face with his hands and cried, "Oy!"

"Are you still alive?" asked the murderer as he shot him a second time. Sheikele fell dead, covered in blood.

The robbers stole the boots and shoes from their dead victims and possessions from the house and then fled.

Seven victims died in this horrible massacre, six of them on the spot. The seventh victim, David Koschevsky, who had just returned to Sokoly, was still alive but gravely injured.

Avrahamel Goldberg, Benjamin Rachlav, and Benyamin Gorkovitz successfully took Feigele away from the Polish family. They drove back to the Surasky house to add Feigele's return to the celebration. When they got to the house, they discovered the six dead victims. David Koschevsky was still alive. They put him in their vehicle and drove him to the hospital in Bialystok, where he died a few days later.

Chaim Tuvia Litvak, the father of two murdered sons—Shammai and Sheikele—started the night as perhaps the happiest person there. His entire family survived and came back to Sokoly. He had three sons and one daughter. Two of his sons were murdered that night. Later, a Polish soldier would murder his third son, Yaakov, in Bialystok. He lost three sons after liberation when they should have all been safe!

The Polish police did nothing about this pogrom and this senseless loss of Jewish lives. No follow-up, no investigation. No arrests. The Russian authorities who then occupied Poland also did not care and did nothing.

After first reading the details of this pogrom, I had to stop writing. I closed my computer. I cried. Then I became angry. These murderers killed seven Jews who had already survived the worst of hell. They would have killed all twenty-one if the gun did not jam, which allowed many to escape. Those who survived had to live with the horrors of this massacre for the rest of their lives on top of everything else they lived through.

After all the horror I had researched and written about to this point, this took me over the edge. I now understood why my parents forgave the Germans, but their hatred toward the Poles (in Poland) lasted their entire lives. For my mother, I now understood the enormous emotional pain she lived with all her life. She lived through the Holocaust and this pogrom from age fourteen to seventeen.

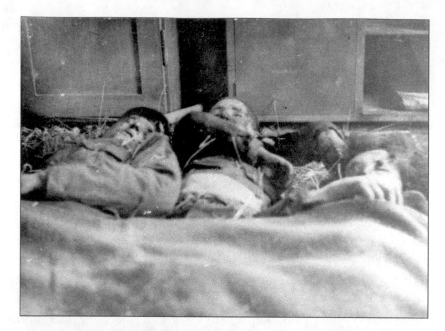

Pictures of the seven murdered in the Sokoly pogrom. May their memories
live on forever.

The pogrom in Sokoly was not an isolated event. As surviving Jews returned to their towns and cities, pogroms were becoming widespread across Poland. Antisemitism was reaching new heights. The Polish Christians took over all Jewish homes and possessions when the Jews were in their ghettos, and the Germans liquidated their communities.

When Jews returned to their hometowns, Polish Christians became angry that any Jews survived instead of celebrating their survival. First, they had no intention of giving up what they had taken from Jews. Second, they supported the Final Solution (Hitler's plan to murder all the Jews of Europe) and expected Poland to be free of Jews. Across Poland, they decided they would finish the job. Attacks and the killing of surviving Jews skyrocketed across Poland. These pogroms confirmed why the Germans built most of the death camps in Poland. They could count on the dedication of Polish Christians to help them with the extermination of the Jews, unlike any other country they occupied.

Adding to the attacks by Poles against the surviving Jews, the occupying Russian authorities looked the other way. Now that the war was almost over, Russian antisemitism became acceptable to Stalin again. He no longer needed the Jews to fight. He had no sense of appreciation for their efforts in the partisans. Returning to ruthless rule was now his primary goal.

Bialystok became a prominent center for Holocaust survivors. Hundreds of survivors from the concentration camps, the partisans, and those who had hidden gathered there. But it did not take long for the plague of robbery and murder of Jews to spread to Bialystok as well.

One morning, a Jewish woman was shot and killed when shopping in the marketplace. Another incident occurred in an alley that led to Jewish shops. Two men wearing Russian army uniforms entered one shop and shot the Jewish shop owner and his wife. They injured the owner and killed his wife.

Other incidents occurred. A group of Jews traveling in a vehicle on the road between Bialystok and Jasionowka encountered robbers disguised as traffic police officers. The robbers stopped them and asked to inspect their papers. They were told to get out of the car and stand in a row. The robbers then shot all of them to death. On this same road, another Jew traveled to sell his house. They shot and killed him.

With all these pogroms and attacks, Jews realized they had to protect themselves. The call went out for former Jewish partisan groups across all Polish towns and cities to form police forces to protect the Jews.

Shmeryl Elman joined to protect the Jews of Bialystok. Shmeryl and the others who volunteered for the Jewish police force patrolled the city in shifts, twenty-four hours per day. They carried weapons, and the Poles were afraid of them. The violence against Jews stopped once these Jewish police groups were in place. Poles, like Germans, were only brave when terrorizing unarmed, helpless people.

After the horrible murders in Sokoly, the Bialystok Jewish Community Committee representatives traveled there. They decided that the last Jews of Sokoly must leave for good. Life in the small towns of Poland was too dangerous, with the gangs of Poles striving to destroy the lives of the returning Jews.

The Jews of Sokoly put the seven dead in a horse and wagon and left for Bialystok, where they thought they would be safer. The Jewish community of Sokoly, which had existed for hundreds of years, had come to a tragic end.

The Sokoly Jews arrived in the Bialystok main square walking aside the horse and wagon carrying the seven dead. Jews in the square watched in shock and disbelief. Shmeryl Elman was there. He and others attended the funerals and helped bury the seven dead souls.

Survivors now knew that remaining in Poland would result in certain death to all of them. Their priority became getting the hell out of Poland as fast as possible.

The Poles did get their wish. They wanted Jews erased from their country. Before the war, there were about 3.5 million Jews in Poland. About 500,000 survived the Holocaust. Thousands more were killed in the pogroms. Then, most of the remaining Jews fled Poland. Today, there are only a few hundred Jews in all of Poland.

In Bialystok, there was an organized effort to capture information and testimony from surviving Jews after they were liberated. Testimony was also collected in other cities where Jews returned. Most survivors had no written record of their experiences—only their memories. Many international organizations placed people in distinct locations to interview survivors while the details were still fresh. The purpose was to collect the stories for the historical record. The information was also used to help survivors determine the fate and locations of family members. Some of this testimony helped identify Nazi perpetrators and track them down.

My mother's youngest sister, Mina, was ten years old when she gave her testimony after the family arrived in Bialystok.

I located this testimony when I searched the archives of Yad Vashem in Israel. I was struck by how Mina shared the details without any feelings and emotions when I read it. It was all matter of fact. Was this because she was still a young child and did not fully understand the horrors she experienced? Or was she blocking out those horrors in her mind? She has since passed away, so that will remain an unanswered question.

Mina's brief testimony was crucial in corroborating the verbal accounts given years later by her sisters, which were from memory and confusing. I had trouble with the credibility of the back and forth with the farmer Kroshevsky. Mina's written testimony in 1945 validated the verbal recollections.

Voivodeship Historical Committee

Bialystok, November 7, 1945

MY EXPERIENCES DURING THE GERMAN OCCUPATION

*Given name Mina Gritczak, born in 1935 in Sokoly, a student at the
Bialystok Jewish school. Survived by hiding in peasants' houses around
Sokoly. Now resides in Bialystok.*

Recorded by Mina herself.

On November 1st, 1942, we were removed from our shtetl, and that day
was the beginning of great adversities. On the first day, my sister and I
stayed in the village. Three days later, she and I met up with our parents and
sister. From that day, we were hiding under oats in a Christian's house. It
was awful because it was easy to suffocate. After seven days of hiding like
this, the Christian told us to leave. We sneaked out into a granary, where we
stayed for two days. When the Christian saw us, he drove us out at once. We
went on our way and laid low in a granary for eleven days without the
Christian knowing. My father obtained food for us. 11 days later, we walked
12 km away from Sokoly. We walked on foot all the way. We were terrified
because we had to walk past a German checkpoint. Not far from there a
Christian took us in. It wasn't bad there for us, and we stayed there for six
weeks.

My father left in search of another place for us because we could no
longer stay there as it was terrifying. Every night, partisans would come and
fire shots all around us. My father secured a place for us in another village.
The Christian came with a wagon to collect us. My mother and I left [on
the wagon] as Christians, while my father and my sister left on foot. We
stayed with the man for three weeks. My sisters were in another village. In
three weeks' time, we went to my sisters. It was on February 1st, 1943.
From that day on, we hid in a Christian house for seventeen months. It
wasn't bad for us there in the first year, but in the second year, we suffered
great hunger.

Toward the end, the peasant didn't want to hide us. We kept reassuring
him that the war would be over soon and stayed until June 1st, 1944. At
the time, there were massive Gestapo raids. The Christian didn't want to
hide us, nor did he want to let us go. He wanted to suffocate us. He took us
to the woods, threw us into a pit, and buried us alive, but miraculously, we
had sticks with us. When we woke up from our sleep, we were already half-
dead, but thanks to the sticks, we were able to make holes to let in some air.

We dug all day and got out in the evening. Upon seeing us alive, the Christian wanted to take his own life because, he said, they would all die because of us. Yet he was afraid to let us go, so he took us back in. The peasant made up his mind to hang us and went about preparing gallows. When the gallows were ready, he came calling us. My father realized the danger and escaped through a hole. That night, I fell ill from fright. My father came back the same night with some goods and money. The Christian agreed to keep us, but it didn't last long, and a few days later we left and hid in a field. As a whole family, we sat in a wheat field, suffering badly from hunger and cold.

At the same time, we learned that the Russians were preparing for an offensive. Later, we heard very frequent shooting, and the Germans started to retreat. Our situation got worse. There was nowhere to go.

One day, when we were all sitting in the wheat field, the Germans appeared, and we ran away. Three days later, we were all reunited. That night, we went up to a field where we ran into partisans. We also managed to escape from there. But my father left us, and we didn't know what to think. We thought they had killed him. Father stayed with a Christian in a different village. Three weeks later, he came back to us. This was three days before the liberation. When Father came back, we were overjoyed.

The Red Army came three days later. We stayed in Sokoly until they killed seven people. Since then, we've been in Bialystok.

Chair of the Voivodeship Historical Committee

13

BUILDING NEW LIVES

The surviving Jews now had two priorities starting with finding a potential spouse. The second was getting the hell out of Poland as fast as possible. As survivors, they knew there were very few Jews left in Europe. They felt a sense of obligation to marry and have children to continue their family lines in memory of the over six million who died. They were also not safe every day they stayed in Poland, and they knew that even if the pogroms ended, their lives as Jews would be worse than before the war.

During this period in Bialystok, Yossel had returned and reunited with Shmeryl. Sheinche met Leibel Wacht, and they married. Shmeryl, then twenty-five, met Rochal Gritczak, then seventeen, and they married. Yossel lived with them.

Rochal and Shmeryl Elman, shortly after being married, 1945

Shmeryl and Yossel received word that their cousin Rivche (Kaplan) Yudevitch and Moishe had survived. They were now in Pruzhany. The Russians would later allow former Polish citizens in Russia to apply for permits to move back to Poland. The cousins filed the paperwork and waited for approval, which took several months.

Only three survivors remained from the European Elman/Kaplan families: Shmeryl, Yossel, and Rivche. Everyone else perished at Auschwitz.

The Gritczak family and a few cousins were the only survivors. The rest of their large families from the Gritczak and Czereczewski sides perished in Treblinka.

From Bialystok, Shmeryl and Yossel wrote a letter to their Uncle Samuel in Syracuse, NY. The letter had a postmark of October 27, 1944. Samuel Elman did not receive it until May 16, 1945. Mail from devastated Europe was slow.

The following is the contents of that letter, which was translated from Yiddish to English upon receipt:

October 27, 1944

Dear Uncle Samuel Elman:

The person writing to you is Shmeryl Elman, the elder son of your brother, Benjamin Elman of Pruzhany.

Dear Uncle, this is the first letter I have written you, and you will certainly wonder why I am the writer of the letter and not my father who always used to write to you.

To my lot has fallen the unpleasant task of letting you know of the sad news concerning the terrible death of my dear parents and sisters who perished amid dreadful sufferings at the hands of the German bandit cannibals, together with all the Jews of the City of Pruzhany.

Of our large family, the only ones remaining alive are my younger brother Joseph and myself. With weapons in our hands, we forced our way through the ghetto fence and fled to the forest and the partisan fight against the bloodthirsty enemy.

During the three years of German occupation, almost the entire Jewish population of Europe was murdered. There remains, perhaps, but one from a city or two from a county.

It is impossible to describe the atrocities of the Hitler bandits in occupied Poland.

Our way of life was a difficult but righteous one. We took revenge on our enemy to whatever extent possible, never sparing our own lives, for revenge was the only thing we could demand for the evil that had been done to our beloved families.

In the twentieth century, an entire nation was put to death by the most horrible inquisition methods, a nation with such fine and beautiful traditions, only because they bore the name of Jew.

We saw in every German the murderer of our loved ones, and at the first meeting, we rendered him harmless.

My brother and I can state with pride that we derived a certain satisfaction in the fact that we eliminated more than one German murderer and revenged ourselves for the innocently spilled blood of our people.

For approximately two years, we lived with the partisans. The life was that of the Middle Ages, a life of hardships. Often, we thought that even in the struggle for existence, such sufferings were not worthwhile. But always, the desire for revenge overcame all difficulties, for other than revenge, nothing remained for us.

Now, after the liberation, we are in Bialystok and are starting a civilized life anew.

To describe all the details of our partisan existence is impossible, for paper is lacking. We hope we can meet you sometime and tell you all about it. We await your reply with impatience.

Best Regards to All Our Family,
Shmeryl and Yossel Elman

After reading this letter, I could not stop thinking about how this letter was the culmination of every horrible experience my father and uncle experienced. I tried to picture my father writing it together with Joe and their emotions. How does anyone sit down and write the first letter telling others that their entire family was murdered in the cruelest of ways? How does one pick up and continue after living such absolute hell? Somehow, the survivors found the strength to do so.

Shmeryl and Yossel were determined to make their way to America to join their uncle and aunts.

Getting to America was no easy accomplishment. America still maintained its immigration quotas by country. Applying for a visa in Poland was not an option given the small quota and large numbers of people who wanted to go there.

After Congress failed to pass an emergency immigration bill, President Harry Truman issued an Executive Order on December 22,1945 requiring all existing immigration quotas be designated for "displaced people." These were people declared "stateless." People had to be housed in a Displaced Persons (DP) camp controlled by Americans for eligibility. They had to have family members in America that would sponsor them and agree to pay for their transportation. The family also had to vouch that they would support the immigrants financially as needed. Back then, there were no government social programs to help immigrants.

The closest area under American occupation was the American Zone in Germany. Munich was the nearest DP camp region. Shmeryl, Rochal, and Yossel left Bialystok for Lodz as the first stop to Munich, Germany. They would receive assistance from Jewish agencies on the ground there.

Zeev, Menucha, and Mina Gritczak remained in Bialystok. Zeev wanted to stay in Poland and rebuild his life in Bialystok. In addition, he did not want to travel, not knowing where they would end up. There was no certainty that the Elmans would make it to America or the Wachts would make it to Palestine.

Leibel Wacht contacted his brother, who moved to Palestine years before the war. He responded and helped them. Sheinche and Leibel then left Bialystok and traveled to Chechnya, then to Berlin. They arrived in the British Zone in Berlin, only to find out the British were not allowing surviving Jews to migrate to Palestine.

The British remained committed to appeasing the Arabs in Palestine, even when facing a situation where Jews had nowhere to go. When Hitler had allowed Jews to leave Germany before 1939, thousands traveled to Palestine by ship, only to be sent back to Germany by the British. Most then perished. Now, after the war, the same thing was happening. Any Jewish survivors who tried to go to Palestine had to do so via illegal ships and get through the British blockade. Most of these ships were caught and sent back.

Uncle Samuel replied to Shmeryl and Yossel's letter from Bialystok. But they were already in Lodz when the reply got to Bialystok. From Lodz, they wrote again to Uncle Samuel and received a response. He told them to stay in Lodz because moving around made it impossible to communicate. Their uncle then began a relentless effort to bring the Elman brothers and Rochal to Syracuse.

They remained in Lodz for a few months and were told to make their way to Munich. The American Joint Relief Agency helped them communicate with their uncle and arrange their travel path to Munich. It was a complicated process under the circumstances. They had to get through the Polish border with Russians guarding it. They then had to get through the Russian-occupied zone in Germany to get to the American-occupied zone.

In mid-1945, the Elmans left Lodz with a group of about fifty other refugees. The relief agency assigned guides to lead them to Munich. They had to travel in secret and cross borders undetected. One significant risk was they had to travel through Russian territory.

From Lodz, they traveled to Vienna, Austria. Then they traveled to Bratislava, Czechoslovakia, and Graz, Austria. They had to cross mountains and rugged terrain on foot for many miles. In late 1945, the group arrived at a camp run by the British for the United Nations Relief Agency. From there, they traveled to the American Zone in Munich, Germany.

They arrived in Munich and found a temporary place to stay. While out walking, Shmeryl ran into a friend from Pruzhany. This friend told him he was staying at an American DP camp named Feldafing. Other people from Pruzhany were already there. The camp still had room for more refugees. He told Shmeryl to join him to visit Feldafing and apply for living arrangements there.

Shmeryl told Rochal and Yossel he would join his friend to check out Feldafing and return to get them once he made the arrangements there.

His friend either did not know or did not tell Shmeryl that applications were required in advance, along with documentation papers. People without documentation had to apply for the documents. They would then be assigned to a DP camp.

When they reached Feldafing, an American MP asked both for their documentation. The friend had his. Shmeryl had nothing. The American MP then treated Shmeryl like a criminal and searched him. He had $60 in American money. Unknown to him, it was illegal for non-Americans to have American money. The MP had Shmeryl put in jail. He could not communicate with Rochal and Yossel. He did not return, and they had no clue what happened to him.

Shmeryl was in jail for about four weeks. Yossel went searching for Shmeryl. He went to Feldafing to inquire. He was told there was no one there named Shmeryl Elman. The person Yossel spoke with looked at the resident list, not the prisoner list. Since Yossel was not asked for documentation and not searched, it appeared the MP who arrested Shmeryl did so out of antisemitism. He probably kept the $60 for himself. They later found out it was not the norm to demand documentation. Most Jews did not have papers. Documentation was needed to apply for residence at DP camps, not to visit them.

Yossel and Rochal worried the entire four weeks Shmeryl was in jail. When Shmeryl returned, he, Rochal, and Yossel completed their applications and received their documentation. Now they could go to Feldafing legitimately. Once in Feldafing, they reconnected with the many survivors from Pruzhany.

With the increasing numbers of displaced people coming into the American zone, the American army opened more camps to accommodate them. One was a camp called Neu Freimann, about ten minutes away from Feldafing. This new camp had larger homes and rooms. It had been a German SS camp. The accommodations were much more comfortable than Feldafing. The Elmans transferred to Neu Freimann.

The Wachts remained in Berlin and then traveled to the American Zone in Munich. They thought they might have a better chance to get to Palestine as refugees under American control. There, they reconnected with Shmeryl, Rochal, and Yossel, who helped them get accommodations at Neu Freimann. They were unexpectedly together again.

Shmeryl and Yossel's cousin Rivche (Kaplan) Yudevitch, and her husband, Moishe Yudevitsh, had a son, Victor, after liberation. They traveled to Munich, arriving at a temporary transit camp inside a large open hall. Their papers were processed, and they then had to wait for an assignment to a DP camp.

A friend of Rivche and Moishe heard they were in the transit camp and visited them. The friend told them many Pruzhany survivors, including their cousins, were at Neu Freimann. This friend then told the Elmans about Rivche and Moishe.

By that time, Neu Freimann was full and not accepting more refugees. Shmeryl and Yossel approached the camp leader to see what could be done to accommodate them there. Moishe had been a Hebrew teacher in Pruzhany. Shmeryl shared this with the camp leader, a young Jewish American soldier from the Bronx. The leader replied the camp needed a Hebrew teacher and admitted Moishe, Rivche, and Victor. The Elmans arranged for their transit. Soon, they were together in Neu Freimann.

Both Feldafing and Neu Freimann housed many Pruzhany survivors, so they became a close-knit group. Most were making plans to immigrate to America, while others, like the Wachts, were planning to go to Palestine. Many survivors chose to go to Argentina, which, in 1945, was already home to 400,000 Jews. And it was far from Europe and the history of antisemitism.

Rochal and Sheinche became pregnant around the same time while at Neu Freimann. The Elmans had a son on August 31, 1946. They named him Benjamin Abraham after Shmeryl and Yossel's father, Binyamin Elman, and their grandfather, Abraham Kaplan.

The Wachts had a son named Abraham the same week, named after Leibel's father. Moishe and Rivche had a second son born there named Harvey.

The Wachts would later travel to Paris. From there, they traveled to Palestine.

Moishe and Rivche, with the help of Moishe's family, received visas to live in the United States. They settled in the New York City area. They assumed the names Morris and Regina Sorid.

Zeev, Menucha, and Mina Gritczak remained in Bialystok until 1951. They then moved to Israel as part of the final exodus of Jews from Poland. They were now together with the Wachts.

Left to right, Yossel, Benjamin, Rochal, and Shmeryl in Neu Freimann DP Camp, 1946

Left to right, Shmeryl & Rochal Elman, Sheinche & Leibel Wacht in Neu Freimann DP Camp, 1945

For most Jewish refugees applying for visas to the United States, the process took time. Still, it was straightforward if you had sponsors who signed affidavits and accepted responsibility for transportation costs, housing, and support. But Shmeryl ran into a significant roadblock.

He had a criminal record because of the American money incident and jailing at Feldafing. The offense made him a criminal. The American Consul in Munich was the sole decision-maker on approving a visa for Shmeryl. He refused to approve a visa because of this.

There was regular correspondence between Shmeryl, his Uncle Samuel, and Samuel's son, Isadore (IJ) Elman. IJ took the lead, using every channel possible to break the logjam. The following are two letters where Shmeryl explained his dilemma to his uncle and cousin in America.

These letters were translated into English as directly as possible from Yiddish upon receipt.

April 4, 1947
Munich

Dear Uncle Samuel,

About our coming to America, I can tell you that my brother, Yossel, will soon be with you. He has already been called to get his visa. You will probably wonder why only my brother and not me? The reason is simple but fatal. As you know, Uncle, in my previous letters, I branded myself with the name "Shlimazel." The "Shlimazel" precedes me wherever I go. The first day that I came to Munich from Austria, I was searched, and they found sixty American dollars on my person. That was enough to arrest me for a month. Now, that is the reason the consul has refused to give me a visa. I had committed a crime against mankind! I could not have American money. Because of me, my wife and baby are also forbidden to leave. They, too, are guilty of the "great crime" I committed.

So, you see, Uncle, my thorny path has not yet ended. I am destined to suffer more. This has been a great shock to us. We had not expected it at all. But what has happened cannot be undone.

Believe me, Uncle, that this whole matter has me confused. The sorrow is greater because the actual murderers of Jews are free and are allowed to go to America. The consul ignores their criminal acts committed during the war. The fact that they killed hundreds of women, children, our mothers, and fathers bothers no one.

I who lost those who are most dear to me; who suffered so much during the past years; was tortured and abused and degraded; utterly despairing many times; for over two years not removing my clothes; who slept in the woods under inhumane conditions both winters and summers, for what reason? Now I have been caught after committing a great crime. I brought sixty American dollars from Poland, not knowing they would forbid it in the American zones. Such a criminal can never go to America!

That is the kind of democracy they preach to us. Perhaps they will reproach me for the crime I committed when I remained alive. According to Hitler's codes, I was not authorized to live. And yet, I am among the living. Perhaps I am still destined to be punished.

Shmeryl Elman

April 19, 1947
Munich

Dear Uncle Samuel,

My wife and small son were called before the consul on April 15th. I, however, delayed their going for a month. About myself, I have already written to you in a previous letter that the consul is not considering. The consul, without even questioning me, has refused to give me a visa. The reason for this is exceedingly trivial but is considered a significant crime here, just as though I had killed many people. However, I am helpless in this matter as we do not have the personnel who could absolve me from my great crime.

As you already know, my crime is that they found sixty American dollars on my person when I was on my way to Munich. That was enough to arrest me for a month and to keep me from going to America. It doesn't help to explain that I brought the money from Poland and was unaware that they forbid it in the American occupation zones. I have no one here that can intervene for me, and those under whose authority this would fall are not interested.

I am more than sure that if someone in the general consul in

Washington intervened, they would do something about my case. That is
why, dear uncle, I am appealing to you. Perhaps an American lawyer could
expedite matters. I hope I will not have to inconvenience you much longer.
    Shmeryl Elman

Samuel and IJ Elman spent an incredible amount of time contacting everyone they could to intervene or influence the American Consul's decision. At one point, Rochal and Benjamin were about to be approved for a visa. They were forced to ask for a delay because they would not travel to the US without Shmeryl. Yossel received his approval for a visa and arrived in the United States in June 1947.

The intense effort by Samuel and IJ Elman, which involved a congressman and other senior government officials, would not sway the American Consul. Shmeryl became impatient and decided to take a different approach.

Sheinche, Leibel, and Abraham Wacht had left for Palestine some time ago. Shmeryl decided to start the immigration process from scratch using the Wachts' identity instead. Stateless refugees had all come to the American zone with no papers and identity. They had to sign affidavits confirming their identity as part of the application process. There was no way to verify those identities. The Elmans became Leib, Sonia, and Benjamin Wacht.

The identity change did work out. The visas for Leib (Shmeryl), Sonia (Rochal), and Benjamin Wacht were quickly approved. On July 8, 1947, they boarded a ship named the *Marine Marlin* for America. Ironically, my birthday is July 8! They arrived in New York City.

USS Marine Marlin docked in New York City

14

LIFE IN AMERICA

Leib, Sonia, and Benjamin stayed for a short time with Sonia's (Rochal's) uncle, Sol Gerstein, in Croton on Hudson. Sol was the brother of Zeev Gritczak and had immigrated to the United States many years before the war. He then changed his name from Gritczak to Gerstein to no longer have a Polish last name. Then they traveled to Syracuse, NY, to join the Elman family. They stayed with Samuel Elman for a brief time until they found an apartment. Yossel also lived with them in the apartment for several years.

They took on English names. Leib (Shmeryl) became Louis. Sonia (Rochal) became Sonia Rachel, and she used Rachel as her everyday name. Benjamin remained Benjamin. Yossel, which translates to Joseph, assumed the name Joseph. Names have always been a confusing process for every generation of immigrants. Some chose names that were direct translations of their native language, while some decided to shorten long names, and others chose new names to represent a fresh start.

Samuel Elman owned a large pants manufacturing company in Syracuse. One of Samuel Elman's sisters, Fanny (Elman) Cooper, married Abe Cooper. Like all family members, she had already been working at the pants factory for years. She met Abe when he was just a street junk peddler, and later, he became extraordinarily successful. During World War II, the scrap business was highly lucrative since scrap was vital to manufacturing all the ships, tanks, vehicles, and equipment for the war effort. So, Abe became wealthy.

Besides his sizable scrap business, he bought a paper mill in nearby Watertown, NY, and other manufacturing companies. With pressure from Fanny, Abe reluctantly helped Samuel Elman sponsor the Elman brothers' visas to America. Fanny became very close with my mother, and to me, she was like a grandmother. Fanny passed away in 1969. She was one of the most loving, kind, and charitable people I have ever known.

Samuel and IJ hired Louis to work at the pants factory. Abe's son-in-law, Harry Marley, hired Joe. Harry managed Abe's Syracuse scrapyard, while Abe focused on his Watertown scrapyard and other businesses.

Joe performed manual labor in the scrapyard, loading and unloading trucks and cutting scrap metal with large shearing equipment. One day, Joe got injured at the scrapyard and broke his ankle. He was in a cast for several months. When Fanny found out, she was upset with Abe because he had put Joe in a dangerous manual labor job. From that point on, Joe worked with Abe at the Watertown scrapyard in a safer position.

Louis's job was to lay out the fabric on the cutting tables. The cutters then cut the material into patterns that moved to the sewing room to sew into pants.

The pants factory was a union shop, and Louis had to join the union. The union workers were unhappy about having the owner's nephew working among them. They viewed him as a spy for management.

The job Louis performed was very boring to him. He was also a very stubborn person in everything he did. Louis watched the cutter closely every day and decided he knew how to cut the material. He stayed in the cutting room during a lunch break and began cutting patterns himself. Louis did not understand union rules, nor did he understand the consequences of violating these rules.

When everyone returned to work from lunch, the cutters saw what Louis had done and reported the incident to the union leader. The union head then determined Louis's actions to be a severe violation of the union contract with the company.

Things escalated to the point where the union leader told Samuel and IJ that the union workers would walk off the job unless they fired Louis. The union leader deliberately escalated things because they did not want Louis working with them. Samuel Elman had no choice but to remove Louis from the union job to keep the factory running.

Louis then became an independent salesman for Elman's pants. He bought an old car and traveled around the Upstate New York area, selling the pants door-to-door. In those days, door-to-door salesmen for all kinds of goods were common, especially in more rural areas where there were no department stores.

Louis had long distances to travel and would leave early in the morning and come home late in the evening. Rachel was not happy with this work. He was only home to eat and sleep, and they had a young son, Benjamin. She also worried about him while on the road, especially in the harsh Upstate New York winters. On one particularly harsh winter day, Louis drove several hours away from Syracuse and lost control of his car on a steep hill. He crashed into another vehicle. It was a nasty accident, and his car got totaled. Fortunately, he only had minor injuries. Rachel had enough and told him he needed to end that line of work.

Over time, Joe had learned much about the operations of a scrap or "junk" yard working for Abe in Watertown. An acquaintance of Joe approached him with an opportunity to buy a small junk business in Syracuse. Joe jumped at the chance with Abe's blessing. Joe and his new partner made a decent living with this business, but after a couple of years, their landlord sold the property, and they lost their lease. They could not find another affordable location, forcing them to close the business.

In 1950, Joe grabbed a ride to visit relatives in New York City and met Edith Rogan. They married and had three children—Cheryl, Marsha, and Barry. Edith passed away in 1999. Joe passed away in 2012.

During this same period, Louis spoke with Harry Marley about a job at the scrapyard. Harry hired him. Louis worked as a manual laborer as Joe had. Harry was harsh and uncaring toward his employees, and Louis felt he was being mistreated.

It was now 1952, and Louis wanted to get out of working for Harry Marley. He pursued getting into the junk business on his own. He discovered another small junk business that the owner wanted to sell. Louis knew of Joe's situation and asked him to join him in buying and running this business together as partners.

From 1952 to 1957, they were partners in this business. They both struggled, but they made a go of it. Then they parted ways, and Joe bought another junk business that was for sale. Both brothers were now on their own.

During this same time a big family feud started. My mother and Edith did not get along, and no one knows the true story behind this.

Over time, this created a rift between Louis and Joe. Joe and Edith were no longer welcome in our house. And, of course, the reverse was true. I was only three years old at this time, and I did not even know I had an uncle, aunt, and three cousins until I was older.

There are different stories of why my father and Joe broke up their partnership or what started this family rift. One version, told by Joe, is that the business did not make enough money for both of them. I am sure they struggled, so this could be true. Another story is that things blew up between my mother and Edith, and my father and Joe got caught in the middle.

Another tale is that Edith interfered in the business, as she did not feel that the money was equally distributed. My father got ticked off and no longer wanted Joe as a partner. Another version is that Joe was dating a survivor my mother really liked. She became upset at Joe when they brokeup. There is also a version that my mother had a strong belief that Holocaust survivors had to marry other survivors. To her and other Holocaust survivors, marriage was not about love. It was an obligation no different from arranged marriages. When Joe married Edith, she got upset with Joe and also held a grudge against Edith. For all I know, there could be even more versions of the story.

Behind the scenes, Louis and Joe still kept in touch through their businesses. I worked in my father's business starting when I was a little kid and through college. In later years, I was the only one he trusted to run it in his absence. So I was there when he and Joe talked on the phone. Sometimes they would visit each other's business and talk. When family members visited our house from out of town, Joe would come over to see them without Edith.

It was awkward when both families were at the same places or events. My cousins and I were strangers. My father and Joe would talk, while my mother and Edith would avoid each other.

When I got older and was on my own, I reached out to my cousins Joe and Edith and developed a relationship with them. I liked everyone, including Edith. What happened was never discussed. I tried to bridge the relationship and see if there could be some reconciliation. I attended my cousin Marsha's wedding around 1981. I would visit a few times a year when my cousins visited their parents in Syracuse. After my parents moved to Florida, Joe and Edith invited me over for Thanksgiving a few times. Joe, Edith, and all my cousins attended Janet's and my wedding in 1983.

When Edith passed away in 1999, I convinced my mother to visit Joe in Syracuse when she came to Rochester from Florida. For a time, they reconnected. Joe would go to Florida for parts of the winter. When he was down there, they would get together.

When my cousin Barry and his wife, June, were married in Washington, DC, in 2000, my family and mother attended. Especially as cousins, we tried to remain connected. But as we all got married, had kids, and lived in different places, we all kind of lost track of each other.

Then in 2002, Joe remarried (another American), and my mother blew up. Once again, my mother wanted nothing to do with Joe from that point on. So, the real story became apparent. It had to be that my mother did not like Joe's choice of American Jews as wives. But when I asked my mother, she denied it and said the new rift was Joe's fault. So, even today, those of us still around have to live with the version of the story we believe.

I believe the version about my mother being upset with Joe for marrying Americans, and I think my mother's insecurity and emotional issues drove this. She always felt American Jewish women looked down on her and did not respect her. How she felt about Joe's choices of wives was no different from how she felt about other survivors who married American Jews. She treated a close friend who grew up with her in Sokoly in the same way. He settled in the New York City area, and once he married an American Jewish woman, the same thing happened with their relationship. We always met him in a restaurant without his wife when we visited him in New York City.

What happened is so unfortunate. There were so few members of my family as it was.

It was on June 23, 1953, that Louis, Rachel, and Benjamin Elman became naturalized citizens of the United States. It was an enormously proud moment for them. My father achieved his lifelong dream of coming to America, joining his family, and becoming a citizen.

Rivche (the Elman brothers' cousin) and Moishe Yudevitsh moved to the United States with their two sons, Victor and Harvey. They assumed the names Regina and Morris Sorid. They deliberately selected "Sorid" as their last name because it came from the Hebrew word *sarid*, which translates to "survivor" in English. Morris once summarized their miracle of surviving as partisans in the forests as follows: "Night turned into day. Darkness was defeated by light. Hope took the place of despair, and the desire to live reigned over resignation."

They settled in Rockaway Beach, NY. Louis and Joe remained close to them. Regina passed away in 1974, Morris in 2013. I remember visiting them at Rockaway Beach many times. They also came to Syracuse occasionally.

As for me, I was born in 1954. I was named after Yaacov Gritczak, my mother's grandfather. Yaacov translates to Jacob in English. Rather than Jacob, I was given Jerry as my first name. I was the only first-generation American in my immediate family. I used to joke with my brother, Ben, about how I could run for president and he could not!

The age difference between Ben and me affected our relationship. We were eight years apart. We shared a bedroom, but I only vaguely recall his time living at home. When I was ten, Ben left for college. He never lived at home or in Syracuse again from that point on. We would see each other during school breaks, and later only for holidays and visits. Our relationship was more like that of distant cousins rather than brothers. I grew up like an only child for most of my childhood that I can remember.

When I was growing up, my father had already become a successful business owner, while Ben grew up with the struggles of being born to an immigrant family who struggled to make ends meet. I grew up spoiled compared to the hardships Ben experienced as a child. My parents lived in an apartment in a rough part of Syracuse for many years. He had to learn how to defend himself with a tough group of kids. I grew up in a new home my parents built in a nice neighborhood. While Ben was growing up, our mother spent a lot of time helping our father in his new struggling business. I grew up with a full-time, stay-at-home mom. Clothing and toys were more challenging to purchase for Ben. I could pick out whatever I wanted (within reason). When Ben turned sixteen and got his driver's license, we only had one family car, and my father had to drive it for work. There were limited opportunities for him to borrow the car. When I got my driver's license, we had two cars. I could borrow a vehicle pretty much whenever I wanted. Ben did not get to go to his first choice for college, even with a sizable scholarship. I got to go to my first choice without a scholarship.

Rachel Elman in front of Syracuse, NY, apartment where Louis, Rachel,
Benjamin, and Joseph lived, 1947

Left to right, Louis, Benjamin, Rachel Elman, 1950

Left to right, Jerry and Benjamin Elman, 1960

Jerry (2 years old) and Louis Elman, in front of new house, 1956

15

THE AMERICAN JEWISH
COMMUNITY DISCONNECT

A fter the war, American Jews gave enormous sums of money to help Holocaust survivors and refugees worldwide.

Over 140,000 Holocaust survivors arrived in the United States between 1945 and 1951. Fifty percent settled in New York City, which became the largest Jewish community globally after the slaughter of the six million in Europe. European Jewish culture, institutions, language, and food thrived in New York City.

The other 50 percent of Jews scattered across all of America. The Jewish communities in these different places were small compared to that of New York City. American Jews in these other communities evolved more toward assimilation and not being labeled as Jews. Increasingly, American Jews were becoming secular and unaffiliated with Jewish institutions. They were moving to the suburbs and out of the old urban Jewish neighborhoods. Most Jews did not speak Yiddish, and there were no neighborhoods and few synagogues that resembled their European communities.

The Holocaust survivors who settled in these other communities were on their own beyond their immediate family members who had sponsored them. American Jews outside of New York City could not relate to or understand the culture and needs of Holocaust survivors. As a result, they came across as unwelcoming. As the survivors arrived, they were foreigners to the local Jews.

As I talk about the disconnect between American Jews and survivors, I am not implying anything deliberate. This attitude came from ignorance. Even within families, this ignorance existed. As an example, Samuel Elman and Abe Cooper were relentless in their efforts to bring their refugee family to America. But when the family finally arrived, they did not know how to deal with immigrant relatives who were different. They viewed them as uneducated and without skills. So, manual labor was to be their career within the companies their uncles owned. They never thought of helping them with education, training, and grooming them for professional positions within their companies. Again, this was not deliberate, rather, it stemmed from difference and misunderstanding.

Many survivors felt that American Jews had little understanding of, or interest in, what the newcomers had recently endured. While American Jews gave sizable sums of money for Holocaust survivor resettlement, a survivor's experience was very distant and abstract to them. Agency workers in Jewish Federations and other support organizations repeatedly urged survivors to put the past behind them and look toward the future. Most survivors, however, needed to speak about the war. They would only do so among other survivors with whom they shared a common language, Yiddish, and the Holocaust experience.

Holocaust survivors were the most successful in adjusting to life in two places, Israel and New York City. Those were the two places that had the highest concentrations of survivors. Israel also had a culture focused on the struggles of war and survival. The War of Independence in 1948, later war threats, border snipers, and terrorist attacks were reminiscent of life in Europe. Jews were being attacked every day.

Even as local Jewish agencies in America claimed far-reaching engagement in the resettlement of survivors, their involvement did not consistently deliver the most compassionate treatment. Active volunteerism was one thing, but personal connection was another. Repeatedly, the newcomers reported a disconnect between themselves and the American Jews who were in roles designed to help them. The lack of connection was true with volunteers and paid professionals who engaged in social services and resettlement.

So, the survivors created their community within a community, much like the "shtetls" (towns) they left. The term for fellow survivors in America was "Greena." Greena is a Yiddish term meaning newbie, settler, pioneer, immigrant, seed. They all had Greena friends, shopped at businesses owned by Greena, and focused on events within the Greena community. There was little participation in the larger Jewish community. They also avoided, or at least minimized, relationships with Gentiles, due to their mistrust of Gentiles and the antisemitism they had experienced in Europe.

All my parents' friends were Greena. None were American Jews. And of course, none were Gentiles. Their closest friends were the family of a survivor they met on the ship that brought them to America. Alex Lyon also settled in Syracuse. Like Uncle Joe, he met his wife on a trip to New York City. Alex married Ann and they had two children, Jack and Esther. They lived about two blocks away from us.

Most survivors joined synagogues as their primary connection to the larger Jewish community. The shul (Yiddish for synagogue) was central to their lives in Europe. They felt more welcomed in the Orthodox (most observant) synagogues, not in Conservative (more modern) synagogues. Greena wanted no part of the Reform movement (the more liberal branch of Judaism). They viewed the Reform movement as trying to mimic Christianity with a strong German influence.

Most of my parents' Greena friends joined the Orthodox synagogue because their prayer style and culture were closer to what they grew up with in Europe. They were also more welcoming to survivors and their children.

My parents joined a Conservative synagogue. I never understood why. I assume it was an effort to be more American. The other kids in the Conservative synagogue viewed those of us who had Greena parents as different. It was hard to make friends. Sometimes I was mocked because of my parents' accents or because my father was a "junkman." Like the adults, the other kids did not understand or know how to embrace immigrants or people who were different. Unfortunately, kids can be cruel, especially in large cliques where the motives are to impress each other at the expense of those outside of the clique. Most of the Jewish friends I had were the children of other Greena, who were friends of my family. I had lots of Gentile friends.

While my parents distrusted Gentiles, they never instilled that in me. They were okay with me having all my Gentile friends. They also understood what I was going through with the other Jewish kids because they had the same experience with Jewish adults. They believed things were different in America than in Europe. Jews were safe in America.

Yiddishkeit is a traditional Yiddish term commonly used in European Jewish communities before the Holocaust. It translates to "Jewish community, values, and culture," combined into one word. European synagogues ensured Yiddishkeit thrived in each community. The Russians and Germans closed all the synagogues as their very first act to disrupt Jewish communities. It is also why they captured and tortured the rabbis.

In Europe, the synagogue was the center of all Jewish life. It was the institution that connected and kept the Jewish community together. Rabbis were the stewards of Yiddishkeit and led modest, humble lives. Rabbis were known as neighbors and friends. They were intimately involved with the joys and sorrows of all their community members. They were the teachers and role models. They were caring and compassionate, and they put others above themselves. Rabbis rolled up their sleeves and jumped in with the physical work to help with community projects, no different from everyone else.

As the survivors came to America, they found the synagogue's role to be much different than it had been Europe. Synagogues in America did not describe their purpose as being the center of Yiddishkeit. Most said their purpose was "prayer and education." As such, the role of the rabbi was far different and even confusing to survivors. Here, a rabbi only "led prayer."

The survivors had to create Yiddishkeit within their groups of Greena friends. If they wanted to pray, they went to the synagogue. If they wanted their children to learn Hebrew and have a bar or bat mitzvah, they were sent to the school in the temple. Community events like celebrating holidays, luncheons, and dinners focused on fundraising, not community building.

To survivors, the way synagogues focused on fundraising, prayer, and education (in that order) was disappointing. Bringing people together to donate money rather than building relationships and celebrating Jewish culture was a very odd concept. I will never forget going to synagogue with my parents for the High Holy Days. There was always a pile of donation envelopes on each seat. The rabbi would ask that everyone fill out and turn in their envelopes before the services even started. All of this annoyed my father.

In religious school, all of us students were constantly bringing envelopes home with us, asking for money for various reasons — after already paying tuition. As a kid, I hated Hebrew school. The rabbis, teachers, and temple staff never seemed to care about us. Kids were viewed as a burden. During services, if we made any noise, we were kicked out. In school, they kept telling us we had to pay attention and learn the material so we would not be an embarrassment during our bar or bat mitzvah. I always felt a sense of fear when at the synagogue. I quit once I had my bar mitzvah. My parents did not try to change my mind. They knew and understood.

Fortunately for my parents, they found a reconnection with Yiddishkeit when they retired to Florida and joined a new synagogue there. We held our daughter's naming at that synagogue.

I am no longer personally affiliated with a synagogue and

expect never to be again. My small group of close Jewish friends are my Jewish community, just like the fellow Greena were to my parents. Every day, I live with Yiddishkeit through these dear friends and family.

My experience with the four synagogues I have been affiliated with is full of disappointment and hurt. I feel compelled to speak out because many other American Jews have had similar experiences. American Jews outside the Orthodox movement are abandoning synagogue affiliation.

My intent in talking about this is not personal. It is a systemic issue. My personal experiences only reinforce the systemic issues. I know there will be people that disagree with me.

Outside of the Orthodox movement, 60 to 80 percent of Jews join a synagogue for the sole purpose of having their children receive the Hebrew education needed to have a bar or bat mitzvah. Once that is complete, they resign. Synagogues were content with this for several generations. As families dropped out, new families with young children joined for the same reason and replaced those that left. Membership remained stable. No growth, no decline. And one must question why the status quo model was accepted instead of doing what was required to grow affiliation. My answer to that is complacency.

The status quo model is no longer viable. Synagogues are seeing major decreases in membership today. Families with young children are not joining in large numbers. At the same time, baby boomers are also dropping out, either by choice or death. Today, it is not unusual for a synagogue to have 40 to 60 percent fewer members than twenty years ago.

It does not have to be this way. I worked with others for many years to organize change within our realm of influence. Sadly, that effort failed. And while I have walked away, it still bothers me. I still see a need for American synagogues to succeed. They need to reassume their significant role in Jewish life. Otherwise, most Jews will become secular over time and lose their connection to any aspects of Yiddishkeit and our past heritage.

I was affiliated with my last synagogue for about twenty-six years. I served on the synagogue board for ten years. I served as vice president of finance for three years and president for four years. I was on the board of a national synagogue organization for two years. I was the synagogue executive director for two and a half years.

It was a toxic work environment, where the focus was on politics, conflict, and hypocrisy. There was childish retaliation against those who pushed back or called out the personal agendas. It affected my emotional well-being. One morning, the verbal abuse was too much. I told them I had enough. I resigned on the spot and walked out of the building.

This internal synagogue hypocrisy is driving American Jews away from synagogue affiliation in record numbers today. Yiddishkeit is not the focus. It is a term no longer used. In many synagogues today, the role of the rabbi is no longer to build community. Many rabbis in America believe they are elite intellectuals entitled to exceedingly high salaries and benefits paid for through ever-increasing annual member dues. It is a country club financial model. Membership is a privilege. The more you pay, the more important you are.

Rabbi salaries and benefits are a secret in most congregations. Why? Because 20 to 40 percent of a synagogue operating budget can go to paying the senior rabbi, 50 to 60 percent to pay all the clergy's salaries. Then, a small percentage goes to paying office staff who are never paid enough.

Rabbis over the past generation have focused on making the job easier for themselves. For many Rabbis, every part of the job is choreographed to do the bare minimum to earn that high pay. In many synagogues, Rabbis have transformed prayer services into a repeat performance. It is like going to the theater to see a show. The clergy performs on stage like actors, only instead of a show, it is called a "service." Sermons are "speeches," most often not personally written but taken off the internet via sermon subscriptions.

Fortunately, there are synagogues out there that are remarkably successful. Yiddishkeit thrives. They are filled every week. It is refreshing to speak with those who belong to these successful synagogues. Their affiliation is an integral part of their lives. They describe it as where they spend time together with their best friends. It is their community, where they have fun. Life would not be the same without this synagogue community. The problem is that these synagogues do not exist in large numbers, and they are only in certain cities.

The successful synagogues will grow as the others shrink and eventually close their doors. New synagogues will evolve following the model of these successful ones. It is only a matter of time.

16

THE POST-TRAUMATIC STRESS DISORDER (PTSD)/SURVIVOR SYNDROME EFFECT

F ollowing their liberation, Holocaust survivors focused on building their new lives, which included a quest for a new home, family, and friends. Most of them suppressed the trauma they endured during the Holocaust, pushing it to the backs of their minds, distancing themselves from the terror and the grief to embrace their new lives.

Despite their best efforts to move on, this facade of wellness eventually gave way to a host of emotional and psychological difficulties for many. Their inability to mourn or acknowledge their suffering led them to show various symptoms. Over time, psychiatrists found and studied these symptoms, grouping them under such names as "survivor syndrome," "concentration camp syndrome," and "PTSD." The trauma of the Holocaust did not end at liberation or leaving Poland. These discoveries came late in the lives of survivors. Most survivors never received treatment.

Psychologists also found a communication pattern in how parents who survived the Holocaust and their children discussed the Holocaust. This communication pattern became known as the "connection of silence." This silent connection became an unwritten understood rule in the families of Holocaust survivors.

Parents never discussed their experience or trauma. Parents disconnected it from the family's daily life to forget and adapt to their new lives after the Holocaust. It was also to protect their children's psyches from harm by depicting the atrocities they experienced.

Holocaust survivors showed remarkable resilience in their day-to-day lives. However, they still suffered from the pain of their traumatic past in various psychiatric symptoms.

Researchers found interesting similarities and differences between Holocaust survivors and control groups they studied:

- Holocaust survivors suffered more psychological trauma and post-traumatic stress than the control groups.
- At the same time, there were no significant differences in cognitive functioning or physical health.
- Holocaust survivors who lived in Israel showed better psychological well-being and social adjustment than survivors who lived in other countries.

Children with depressed parents are two to four times more likely to develop depression before adulthood. Extensive research has also shown that a mother's depression (especially when untreated) can interfere with her child's social, emotional, and cognitive development.

Like most survivors' homes, my parents rarely talked about the Holocaust. It was an unwritten rule not to ask about it. My father never shared the written documents he kept. The few pictures of the family they preserved were never shown to us other than pictures on their bedroom dresser. My brother and I did not know my father did a Shoah project video interview until he died in 1989; we found it going through his things. Only then did we get to see it. But he was dead. We could not ask him questions.

My mother refused to document anything, and she declined to be interviewed for a Shoah video. When she died, she only passed on pictures of her family and a few friends in Sokoly.

My parents also never talked about any of their feelings and emotions. I learned never to talk about mine. Feelings had to be encased with concrete and steel. Today, I understand why. They wanted to avoid hurt and pain. Opening up to others could lead to betrayal. Becoming emotionally close to others opened the door to vulnerability. It opened the door to unlocking feelings that they hid and buried. It opened the door to making their children weak. Controlling one's emotions was a sign of strength for Holocaust survivors. For many, that ability was the very reason they survived.

My parents never embraced each other in public or in front of my brother, Ben, and me. I never saw them hug, kiss, or hold hands. This behavior got passed on to me, and I behaved the same way for years. Embracing others was very awkward for me for a long time. It made me feel scared for reasons I could never understand.

Both my parents believed in total self-dependence. Ask no one for a favor. Borrow nothing. If you did, you then owed someone something in return. Depending on anyone else makes you vulnerable. That was their life experience during the Holocaust. I own virtually every tool on the face of the earth because I will not borrow anything! To this day, it is tough for me to ask for help or borrow something.

When comparing their feelings and emotions, my father and mother were two different people. My father never looked back on anything. The future mattered to him, not the past. He displayed no bitterness or anger about the Holocaust. I was close with my father. I enjoyed spending time with him. He was someone I always looked up to as my role model.

In doing the research for this book and through a discussion with a close friend, I realized my father was able to mourn his losses and have closure. His diary highlights just that. His ability to fight in the partisans and seek revenge brought him closure. Knowing he saved the lives of many other Jews brought him closure. Knowing that his effort helped defeat the Germans brought him closure. Surviving and raising a family brought closure to him.

For my mother, it was the opposite. The trauma remained with her for the rest of her life. She could never find a release for her emotional pain and suffering. With each tragic moment of her experiences during the Holocaust, she faced more tragedy and emotional distress. There was never a time for her to process what had happened, mourn her losses, and bring closure. Over time, the emotional scars consumed her.

My mother was close with Ben. He was born in the DP camp in Germany. There was always a difference in her relationship with me—a first-generation American. I was not part of the past. I had not faced the hardships Ben did in those early years. He made some of the journeys with her through that secret past. I did not.

My mother was a full-time homemaker. She cooked and cleaned all day. Every room in the house was cleaned every day. And if a room got used again, it would get cleaned again. The living room was only for company. I would get in trouble if I ever went into the living room and sat on the couch or a chair.

She also had eating habits that were driven by her survival experience. While she cooked every meal at home, she never made her own plate unless we had company. She always placed more food on our plates than most of us could eat. She would sit at the table without a plate of food while the rest of us ate. Then, as we could not finish what was on our plates, she would grab each plate and eat the leftover food alone before washing the dishes. If there were just bones leftover, she would chew them for any remaining meat.

She often just ate bread. She would always claim she loved bread and needed nothing else. Of course, this came from surviving on scraps of food, usually only bread, while hiding in the barn during the Holocaust.

She was a food hoarder. We had cabinets and shelves built in the basement that she would fill with canned and boxed food— enough to last for months, even years. She bought meat in bulk (an entire side of butchered meat) and always had a big chest freezer in the basement filled with beef. It would continually get replenished long before it was near empty.

The hoarding stemmed from the hunger she lived through during the Holocaust. She lived with this subliminal fear that something terrible would happen and we would starve. She always remembered being that young girl with the braided hair, risking her life to beg for food. To avoid hunger, we had to have our "strategic stockpile" of food.

I thought about her during the COVID-19 pandemic. The supermarkets ran out of paper products and food, and it was hard to get lots of things for a long time. Perhaps this was an example of the kind of crisis she feared.

In my early childhood, my relationship with my mother seemed normal. As a full-time homemaker, she was home with me every day. She would play with me. I remember watching the popular soap opera of that time, *The Edge of Night*, with her when I was young. Once or twice a month, we would take the bus downtown to shop. I always got my favorite lunch—a burger, fries, and a Coke—at the restaurants in Woolworth's, McCrory's, and other downtown diners. She was the one to sign me up for summer camp, which I loved.

On my first half-day of kindergarten, my mother rode the bus with me and stayed outside my classroom while I was in class. Then she rode the bus home with me. I did not feel embarrassed because I thought it was supposed to be that way. None of the other kids made fun of me or made an issue about that first day of kindergarten.

She encouraged me to be active with everything in school in those years. I was in the band, orchestra, choir (I could sing very well until puberty!), and many other activities. Elementary school was my happiest time growing up. I fondly remember those days. But then, things changed.

I turned thirteen in July 1967. My parents had decided years before that my bar mitzvah would be in Israel. The Six-Day War started in early June. We expected the war would cancel our plans and began making alternative arrangements in Syracuse. It was a short war. The situation in Israel quickly returned to normal, and travel was reopened within two weeks. Our original plans remained unchanged.

My bar mitzvah was a family reunion and a reunion of all the survivors from Pruzhany and Sokoly who moved to Israel.

One of my aunts, Sheinche, had visited the United States the year before, so I had already met her. The rest of the family were strangers to me. I met my grandparents, Zeev and Menucha, aunt Mina, uncles Leibel, Yitzchak, cousins, and the whole extended family in Israel. Back home, I had a tiny family. In Israel, I had a large family. My mother and I spent the entire summer there. My father came for two weeks because he could not leave his business for longer than that.

My brother, Ben, could not attend. During his junior year in college, he was in Hawaii and Taiwan as part of a unique exchange program. He did not get back until the end of the summer. That year in Asia changed his life and led to his distinguished academic career in Asian and Chinese studies at Princeton University.

I had a wonderful time connecting with family I had never met. I loved the time in Israel. All my relatives were so welcoming, and I became close with them within this brief time. I cherished being with my grandparents. The summer flew by, and soon, it was time to return in late August to go back to school. Coming back home seemed weird. A big family no longer surrounded me anymore. I felt lonely at first. Then school started, and I went back to my everyday life.

Bar Mitzvah in Israel, 1967 (Left to right) Rachel Elman, Menucha and Zeev Gritczak, Jerry and Louis Elman

My extended family in Israel, 1967

The trip to Israel triggered a dramatic change in my mother's behavior. The Vietnam War was underway. President Johnson ended the graduate school deferment, which affected Ben. He was finishing undergraduate school in May 1968, and he had plans to go to graduate school. My mother was now terrified that Ben would get drafted, sent to Vietnam, and killed. That truly scared the hell out of her. But something bigger was also going on. The trip to Israel seemed to change her.

When we returned from our trip, her depression worsened. She became much more bitter, angry, and lashed out at me for all kinds of things. I could do nothing right. All the things she accused me of doing wrong were also on purpose in her mind. I was selfish. I was spoiled. I was lazy. I was careless. I was not smart. My grades were never good enough. I had it too good. I had too much fun. I did not know what actual suffering was. She often called me a dummy. Every day I came home from school, she started arguing over something. She never asked how my day in school was. I was her punching bag.

I solved the daily argument problem by not coming home from school until my father got home from work. I went to friends' houses. I stayed at school for activities. I rarely had friends come to my house. When my father was home, my mother was different. She left me alone. My father never got to see the conflict between my mother and me directly. I never talked to him about it. But over time, he began to realize what was happening.

My mother also became incredibly sad. She would shift from moods of bitterness to sadness. She often became obsessed with the past and could not look forward. She would talk bitterly about the life she was denied. Sometimes she said she wished she had not survived. She would say, "I survived. For what?" She begrudged and badmouthed (behind the scenes) people who lived fun lives and were happy. She felt that being a survivor meant living a life of unhappiness and guilt.

She also missed her family, who were all in Israel. That added to her depression. Our visit to Israel worsened that. I think if it had been her choice, she would have preferred joining her family in Israel rather than coming to the United States.

In 1980, my father sold his business. My parents moved to Florida later that year. I found out after they moved that my mother did not get together with or say goodbye to any of her friends in Syracuse, even her closest friends. Several of her friends contacted me after they heard my parents had moved. Some wanted to know if she was mad at them. Others were a bit angry and hurt. I did not get it either at the time, but I did not throw her under the bus. I told her friends that goodbyes were difficult for her. It was not personal. Goodbyes are awkward for everyone.

Today, we know that goodbyes can be very traumatic to survivors. They never got to say goodbye to their grandparents, parents, siblings, cousins, nieces and nephews, their closest friends, their entire community. They never even had the opportunity to mourn those losses. So, while I did not understand it then, I know it now. To her, there was too much sorrow and pain associated with goodbyes. So, she just left.

Looking back, I realize my mother lived through emotional hell. Today, it is obvious my mother suffered from severe depression and PTSD. She needed help. She was ill.

Going back to the family rift of the 1950s and her relationship with my Uncle Joe, her emotional illness controlled her. To her, survivors married other survivors out of obligation, not choice or love. Her experiences with American Jews were not good. She always felt American Jews, especially women, looked down on her as a survivor. Much of that was her insecurities. But in fairness to her, much of that was driven by her experiences with the American Jewish community. She always felt she never met the standards of the American women in our synagogue. And frankly, many of the women in our synagogue treated her in ways that made that real. I know I felt the same way in how I was treated. Had my parents joined the Orthodox synagogue, her relationship with American Jews may have been different. But even that would not have healed the emotional demons that consumed her. Her life would have been so different had she received the help she needed.

17

MY DEPRESSION

The book *Children of the Holocaust: Conversations with Sons and Daughters of Survivors* by Helen Epstein, published in 1979, made the then astounding claim that the severe trauma of the Holocaust and the psychiatric symptoms of survivors had been passed on to their children—a generation that was not even alive during the war. I read the book when it was published because I knew I was suffering from psychological and emotional issues related to my parents' experiences. In reading that book, I realized I was not alone. Unfortunately, I read the book ten years after beginning my battle with depression.

Within six months of our return from Israel, my emotions and personality started changing. The change started with a constant feeling of stress. Then I started having stomach problems and headaches. The doctors performed tests and could find nothing wrong. They said I was going through puberty and stress from school. I lost interest in the things I used to love to do. I had been outgoing, but I became a shy introvert. I became my biggest self-critic. I developed a sensitivity to criticism, rejection, or failure. Once, I tried to run away from home. In later years, I often thought about suicide. I never tried, but I thought about it.

I also started having regular nightmares, consisting of different situations where people were chasing me, wanting to beat me, shoot me, or stab me. They are hard to describe, but they were like TV and movie episodes of people fleeing the bad guys. I would then start screaming, and if I did not wake up and stop, my wife, Janet, would jab me in the side! I do not have nightmares that place me in the Holocaust. The nightmares have become much less common since completing years of therapy. The nightmares represent the emotions and a buried sense of fear I developed from my parents' PTSD. It plays out in my world, not the Holocaust.

Over time, I morphed into a different person. I was not happy. I built up this thick armor. No one, including myself, would know what was going through my head. No one would see the anxiety and self-doubt I felt. Like an actor, I would play the part of a normal person, keeping complete control of all my insecurities. I pretended to be happy, but I was beating myself up mentally when I was alone. I would revisit my day, thinking about everything I should have said or done differently. Everything I did focused on exceeding the expectations of others, having other people say I did good! Nothing was about me. I also had this voice in my head reminding me to feel guilty whenever I had fun. I dealt with that voice by becoming an overachiever. Living a life focused on work minimized the time to have fun and feel guilty.

The emotional game of keeping everything inside and acting normal and happy worked until my junior year of college. The stress and energy of keeping my emotions inside then became too much. I was overwhelmed and mentally exhausted. I felt physically ill. My grades crashed for the first time in my life. I was thinking about dropping out of school. What kept me in school at that time was the guilt of wasting my father's hard-earned money if I dropped out. I would also be admitting failure, something I could never do.

My major was electrical engineering, and for an elective, I became interested in psychology, most probably to figure myself out, like so many others who take psychology. I took a psychology class that semester, and I spoke with the professor to see if he could guide me.

I scheduled a time to meet in his office, and I shared what was going on and how I felt. He asked some questions, and we talked about things I had never talked about before.

He told me I needed professional help, and he also said that I knew that already. He was right. I did. He said he could help, but there was a conflict and ethical issue for him to counsel me because I was a student, and he was a professor.

He referred me to a colleague who was a psychiatrist and professor at the University of Rochester School of Psychiatry. I began seeing this psychiatrist weekly, and it helped. He helped me understand that I had embedded my mother into my head and allowed her to control me mentally and emotionally. I began to realize that the constant desire to please her drove my thinking and actions. When she was not around, I would beat myself up mentally in place of her. I had to live a life of suffering out of obligation, just like her. But we never got into the part of understanding why my mother behaved like this. The focus was getting her out of my head.

The therapy helped. I could again pretend to be normal and happy. I could now replace the padlock on my feelings and control them again. I still did not face all demons, deal with them, and fully recover. Against the advice of my psychiatrist, I decided I was "well enough" at that point and did not need any more counseling.

I graduated the following year and started my professional life as an engineer. I was successful and eventually landed the job I had always wanted at Eastman Kodak Company. Back then, everyone in Rochester, NY, wanted to work for Kodak. It was not easy to get in. I rose through the ranks successfully and enjoyed my work until later years when poor management ran the company into the ground.

I married my wife, Janet, in 1983. Our son, David, was born in 1987; our daughter, Sandi, in 1991. After my father sold his business and retired in 1980, my parents moved from Syracuse to

Florida and resettled there. While my parents would visit us and we visited them, my relationship with my mother was still the same. We did not like each other, and we never got along.

In September 1988, my father had a cerebral hemorrhage. He never recovered. While he was not in a coma, he could only move his eyes around. He could not communicate, and he could not move. He would sometimes attempt to move his lips, but he could not. We had no idea if he was aware of things. If he was, it had to be absolute hell for him. He spent three months in a treatment facility and then moved to a nursing home. My mother was with him every single day from early morning to evening. He passed away in October 1989, at the age of seventy. In his last ten years, he aged. The toll of the Holocaust and his demanding work in his business showed. It shortened his life. My father's death hit me hard, but I would not let my emotions out. Looking back, I did not deal with mourning his loss. I blocked it.

After my father's death, whenever my mother would visit us, or vice versa, we got into worse arguments. But now, it was me starting them. I kept my grief and emotions about my father's death locked up. My release was being mean to her. At that point, I blamed her for all my problems, just like she blamed me for hers.

I never tried to influence her relationship with David and Sandi. Ironically, things repeated themselves. My mother adored David and would shower him with affection, but she never became close to Sandi and seemed to shun her. It was like my brother and me all over again in the next generation.

In the year 2000, I was heading for another emotional crash, but this time, I knew it. Kodak was in a tailspin. I reported to the worst manager I ever had in my career. The project I was working on was a management disaster from the start, destined to fail. Janet and I were having conflicts. She could never understand why I could never "open up," and her questions started reminding me of the constant criticism from my mother. She started pushing my "hot buttons," and I would react. That was not good for either of us. I was stressed out, exhausted, and I felt a meltdown coming. I knew enough from the last time that I could not let that happen and needed help. My primary care physician put me on anti-anxiety medication to provide immediate help. He also referred me to a new psychiatrist.

This time, I received both counseling and specific medication geared to the depression I suffered. The medication had a faster effect, but the counseling was effective over time. This time, we removed the padlock and peeled back all the armor. I started to understand what was inside my head, the triggers, and what I needed to change regarding my thinking and behaviors. It took a couple of years to make considerable progress. I also learned and understood why my mother behaved the way she did. For the first time, I realized it was not me! She was ill. I came to peace with myself and her.

I was fortunate that while I had depression and my mother significantly influenced my emotions and thinking, so did my father. Even with my insecurities and emotional problems, I have always been goal-oriented and forward-thinking like him. I am stubborn and determined, like him. I always had a destination I wanted to reach and never gave up. Another thing he taught me was to confront my fears. Doing that minimizes the pain. The example he gave was going into the chilly water. Many people hate the cold and go into the water slowly, suffering the pain of the frigid water with each move. Those who confront the chilly water jump in, and the pain is quickly over, replaced by feeling refreshed. Even with depression, I faced the non-emotional things that I feared. I always jumped into the water. I was terrified of public speaking and knew that I had to overcome that to achieve my career goals. I had to jump in the water. So, I took Dale Carnegie and other public speaking classes. That part of my father's influence helped me successfully get through life, even with the anchor of depression holding me down.

My father also gave me a solid ethical compass. He always did what was right, no matter the consequences. He instilled that quality in me. As I look back at my life, I have never sold myself out and have always stood up for what is right, even when doing so has had negative consequences.

One thing I have learned about depression is that it rewires your brain. You can never get all the wiring back to what it was. Like other therapies and addiction, you manage things but never fully recover. You learn there is only one person who controls your feelings and behaviors, and that is you. But you must keep working on it. At best, you can minimize depression, or it lies dormant, as it can come back at any time. And when it does, you must deal with it, or it will overwhelm you again. There are still days when I feel depressed. There are days I still feel unhappy. But I catch it and snap out of it. I know I must jump into the chilly water and get rid of the fear and discomfort. I know I can manage it today.

As much as I try, there are two sensitivities I will never overcome. One is being micromanaged. The other is being with anyone who unjustly and constantly criticizes and finds fault with others, including me. No matter how hard I try not to let those sensitivities get to me, they always will. My brain is wired to push back and fight whenever I hear or perceive someone treating me or others like my mother did. That is one scar that will never heal.

My life would have been different had I understood my mental health earlier and received help earlier. I do not regret my life; I would not be who I am today without it. What I do regret is not spending more time with my family. Janet, David, and Sandi deserved more of my time and engagement. My overachiever mindset made work and other things a higher priority too often.

I also made a foolish, impulsive business decision after volunteering to be laid off at Kodak in 2006. I bought a used car sales and repair business in 2007. I was always a car enthusiast. Being in the car business was a dream I had had for many years. That is an extremely high overhead business. Car sales declined nationwide, and I did not see the 2008 economic crash coming. To keep the doors open, I incurred a large amount of debt. I almost lost everything.

The stress I felt was overwhelming, but I did not feel broken. One day, I was sitting in my office, figuring out what bills I could afford to pay. My mother came back to mind. I thought about her comments that I did not know real suffering and enduring extreme hardship. At that moment, I realized she was right. I never really did until then. Even fighting depression was not anywhere close to fixing that business mess. I began to think of it as my battle as a partisan. It was my battle for survival. Instead of thinking about bankruptcy, I focused on the things in my control to turn the business around. The determination my father instilled in me kicked in.

I beat the near-impossible odds of turning that mess around. In 2018, I was able to sell the business. In the end, I came close to at least breaking even for the eleven years of effort I put into it. That was a win. That was my "miracle through hell"! Somehow, that unwise decision was meant to be. I did have it too good for most of my life. That experience tested me to my limits. I now understand suffering and genuine hardship in ways I never had before. My mother was no longer alive during this time, but I believe she would have been proud of me.

Louis Elman sixtieth birthday, June 1979

Left to right, Rachel, Benjamin, Louis, Jerry Elman with our 1970s look,
June 1979

18

THE BEST DAYS WITH MY MOTHER

As my depression improved from my treatment and therapy, my relationship with my mother improved. She did not change, but I did. I just let things go. I understood her depression and that what she said and did to me and others over the years was not deliberate. She was ill. I felt terrible for her. I now knew she needed therapy and medication. I told her that, but she would not have it. In her mind, there was nothing wrong. Another time, she told me it was too late, and she was too old.

In May 2004, doctors diagnosed my mother with lung cancer. She never smoked. Her father did back in Sokoly. Was that the trigger or something else? We will never know. They put her on a new medication developed for her type of lung cancer. The treatment seemed to work; her tumor was shrinking. But she also had a history of heart issues. Within a couple of months, she had fluid in her lungs, and we knew her heart was giving up on her.

During my visits to her home in Florida, my mother was a different person. We had wonderful conversations. She genuinely cared about me. We talked about personal stuff for the first time. Visits used to be her cooking our favorite Jewish foods from scratch for days. When I arrived for my first visit, she made some food, but not the big spread she usually did. We only ate at her home one evening. She wanted to go out to eat each of the other nights. She was a lot more relaxed and talkative. And while seriously ill, she seemed incredibly positive, which was quite different from her usual bitterness. In the past, when we went out to eat, we would eat the meal, talk a bit, and then leave when we were done. There was rarely anything to talk about without an argument. After eating, we had an enjoyable conversation and stayed for a while.

Her doctor told me she was receiving depression medication with her cancer treatments. The doctors recognized that she suffered from depression. Her state of mind was an essential part of beating cancer. Over the next few months, I made several more visits to Florida. At that point, she did not cook anything special at all. All our dinners were out at restaurants. A few times, we stopped at the mall after eating. She had no interest in shopping for herself, which was unusual. She only wanted to go to the men's department and look at clothes for me. We both had a wonderful time together, every visit.

Still, it was evident that she was getting weaker, even as the tumor got smaller. The last time we went out to eat and went to the mall, we did not walk far. She asked me if it would be okay if we went home. She said she was tired. That was a change because she would never ask me if doing anything was okay in the past. She would tell me what she wanted to do—period. I drove back to the condominium, and she went to bed early. Both Ben and I had no clue that her heart was getting weaker; it was not the cancer itself. I had to leave the next day, not knowing the night before would be our last time going out anywhere together.

It was now late September of 2004, and Ben was visiting her. I had scheduled to go down to Florida two days later. Ben called unexpectedly and told me she had a heart attack while walking back to her condominium from the car. She collapsed, recovered, and was very weak. She was taken to the hospital. There was nothing more they could do for her. They admitted her into a hospice that same day. The doctors said she had a couple more weeks. Ben took his scheduled flight home once she was situated in hospice. I was already on a plane heading down. When I arranged my flight, I decided I would stay until she passed away, hoping it would be later rather than sooner. That was a big sign of recovery for me. In the past, I would have been too concerned about work and would have never told my boss, "I don't know when I will be back." I stayed connected with work remotely, but my mother was my top priority.

The remaining time was the best I ever had with her. We talked about her life, and the hurt inflicted on her from the Holocaust. She understood and apologized for how she treated me all those years. We both cried and hugged each other. It hurt me to see her emotional recovery while she was dying physically.

One late morning, I was with my mother in her room, and she started having intense pain and chest convulsions. Alarms were going off, and the nurses and doctors rushed in with a crash cart. They injected something into her using a giant syringe. She quickly stabilized. The doctor told me she had just had another heart attack. She was stable but much weaker. She now only had days left. She was alert and could talk. She told me she wanted to spend her last days in her own home. The hospice staff said it was doable, but only if I could arrange for twenty-four-hour medical aid coverage for her. They would supply a hospital bed and arrange for nursing and medication coverage. I made all the arrangements. In the meantime, Ben was on an airplane and would arrive in the evening.

The next day, she was home. She got stronger at home, which amazed the aides, visiting nurse, Ben, and me. A couple of days went by, and she seemed stronger. Ben had something important at work and traveled back. We both believed she would continue for a few more days. I thought she would intentionally hold on until Ben returned. That afternoon, Ben flew out.

The following morning, she was alert and feeling stronger. We were talking and joking. She was in a great mood all day. It was the best day I ever spent with her. It was getting into the evening. I had not eaten dinner yet and was staying at a hotel. The aide was staying in the guest room, so I stayed in a hotel the whole time my mother was back home. We hugged and kissed, and I told her I would be back in the early morning.

At about 11:00 p.m., I received a call at the hotel. The aide told me things had changed. I needed to get back there as soon as possible. It was about a fifteen-minute drive. I walked into the condominium, and the aide said, "I am sorry," and I saw my mother lying on the bed, now in peace. She had passed away in her sleep. The aide called me right away but did not want to upset me with the news until I was there. I cried in a way I had never cried before. I hugged and kissed my mother. The aide had already called the hospice to send the nurse back. She could not be officially declared dead until someone from the hospice did so.

I called the funeral home to come to pick her up. She had made all her arrangements years before. Then I called Ben. The nurse arrived quickly. He declared my mother dead at 11:55 p.m. I looked at my watch, and the date caught my eye. It was October 12, 2004. My father passed away on October 12, 1989. My mother chose to pass on the same day as my father, and they were now together again.

The funeral home staff arrived and moved her into their van. I walked alongside her as they put her in their van. I told the aide to spend the rest of the night there, and I headed back to the hotel. My mother's death hit me worse than the death of my father. I was up most of that night in tears.

My mother's funeral took place two days later. I have missed her ever since, along with my father. I think about the two of them daily.

Left to right, Janet, Louis, Jerry, Rachel Elman, August 1988 Our last
picture together before Louis's cerebral hemorrhage one week later

David with his grandmother, November 2003

Last picture of the entire family together with Rachel Elman, November 2003 Left to right, Janet, Sandi, Sarah and Benjamin Elman, Jerry, David and Rachel

THE MYTH THAT JEWS DID NOT RESIST

If my father were still alive, he would insist I include this chapter in this book. The images of the death camp, pictures, videos, and later movies that depicted Jews as being passive and allowing themselves to be slaughtered always struck a nerve with him. Yes, there was the Warsaw ghetto uprising, but that is depicted as a unique one-off uprising, not the norm.

Even I believed the images of the Jews passively walking to their death and destruction without any attempt to fight or resist. I could not understand how they could just allow the Germans to slaughter them. But I did not know my parents' stories. I did not know or understand what a partisan faced and accomplished. I just viewed what both of my parents did as ways to survive, not resist.

My father always said that these images did not accurately capture what was going on behind the scenes. When my brother and I both asked my father the question, "Why didn't the Jews resist?" he could not answer it in a discussion. He felt compelled to write the answer. At the time, I did not understand why he did that, but today, I know. The answer was not just meant for his sons. It was meant to reconcile the conflict and guilt he carried with him. Was leaving his family and joining the partisans the right thing to do? Should he have stayed with his family till the very end? He finally dealt with the conflict and guilt that still haunted him in writing his answer. He shared the questions that went through his mind as he faced deciding to leave. After reading his response, I realized that writing about this question was therapy for him. It was a cathartic experience for him.

The reality is that resistance took place every day, in every way possible. These acts of resistance were not captured in pictures, nor could they be documented. They all happened in secret, undercover. Any other way would have flagged the Germans.

The German policy of collective punishment was the most effective tool to prevent Jews from openly resisting or fighting back. Even the Warsaw Uprising started when the Warsaw ghetto was being liquidated. There was no reason to fear collective punishment at that point.

If one Jew did anything wrong, the Germans would execute their entire family. They even killed whole villages for the act of one Jew. No one wanted to do anything to cause such mass killings in every Jewish community.

The Judenrat of all Jewish ghettos performed all kinds of discreet acts of resistance. The establishment of illegal markets and bribery allowed the Jews in most ghettos to have adequate food, medicine, and housing. Without this, life would have been far more miserable. The smuggling of weapons, building bunkers to hide food and supplies, and building tunnels for the future escape were all secret, organized forms of resistance.

Jews countered the Germans and their collaborators in other ways. Smugglers sent children to safety, and couriers carried messages between the ghettos. Forgers created documents to ensure safe passage to non-occupied countries. They made fake identity cards that allowed Jews to "pass" as non-Jews.

Jewish workers sabotaged weapons they put together or repaired for the Germans. Many Jews had jobs manufacturing munitions and bullets. They made sure a high percentage were defective. Their lives were at risk if they got caught, and in most cases, they were not. Because of them, German weapons and ammunition were faulty while fighting on the front.

Because of German collective punishment, Jews would only resist in quiet, behind the scenes ways. Ways that would not catch the attention of the Germans. Most communities planned to only resist openly and in large numbers when the end was absolute. At that point, they had nothing to lose.

Jewish resistance was significant in other passive ways. The Germans forbade the practice of Judaism along with any form of Jewish education. Spiritual resistance took the form of secret prayer services and teaching children to read Hebrew throughout the occupation of the ghettos. Artistic resistance produced art and poetry in ghettos and camps. Even when walking to the gas chambers in the death camps, Jews refused to show fear and cowardice to the Germans. That is why the pictures show passive compliance.

Without taking up arms, Jews stood in defiance to the Germans right up to the very end of their lives. The Germans could not take away their dignity and self-respect as they facilitated the killing process in the camps. And even in the camps, underground economies appeared, sabotage of equipment happened, children were hidden or given to Christians to protect. And many escaped the death camps in the most clever and brave ways.

When asked about Jewish bravery and resistance during the Holocaust, survivors are almost unanimous. They will say that it took more courage to be herded into the cattle cars, live in the death camps, and march to the gas chambers than fight as partisans.

My father wrote the following as his answer to this question around 1975. He wrote it in English, so no translation was required.

My youngest son asked many times why the Jews allowed themselves to be led to slaughter. Why did they not resist the Germans when they knew they would be massacred, that the end was near? Why? Why? Why? People never stop asking this question.

While the question is easy to ask, the answer is complicated and comes from living through the horrible experience. The answer is obvious only to those who survived.

Imagine that as a Jew, your life had little value to the Germans and your non-Jewish neighbors who knew you. Betrayal was common. Jews were turned over to the Germans for as little as a loaf of bread, a pound of sugar, a pound of flour, or even less, as a reward. Many Jews were turned in just for the satisfaction of knowing they would be killed.

Imagine knowing the people who were your neighbors deliberately sending you to certain death for a loaf of bread and the opportunity to loot and even take over your house.

Today, this question is being asked by physically and mentally healthy people who are not hungry, have shelter, clothes, friends, and can go and do anything they want. They have dreams they know they can pursue. No one has marked them for death. They live as respected members of their community. They have not faced the most inhuman treatment one can ever imagine. The destruction of one's self-esteem. Made to believe they are garbage to be destroyed. Live caged up in ghettos. And on top of all this, certain death is the outcome for all.

People had to make choices under circumstances no one asking the question has ever experienced and can even imagine. The Germans branded the Jews with Stars of David, starved them, experimented with them, took the gold and silver out of their teeth, worked them as slave labor, exposed them to the worst sanitation conditions, herded them into fenced in ghettos, and shot anyone who was not where they belonged. They performed daily mental and physical torture. They separated families and took children away. They randomly shot Jews to death just to make an example of them.

The most effective weapon the Germans used to prevent Jews from fighting back was collective punishment. If one Jew did something perceived as resistance or fighting back, entire families, even an entire community of Jews were killed, not just the one perpetrator. No one wanted to be responsible or face the guilt for the death of others in their family and community because of their actions.

Many Jews, especially the heads of families, were emotionally destroyed because they could do nothing to protect their families. Any attempt to protect them was a sure death sentence for all. And doing nothing was also a sure death sentence for all. Many fathers, including my own, chose the path of suicide out of the guilt and feeling of hopelessness that they could do nothing to keep their family members from harm and death. My father chose the path of suicide, like so many others, because he could not face seeing his family slaughtered, knowing he could do nothing to save them.

My father knew that my brother and I were planning to flee. He told us it was a futile effort. Where would we go? Germany controlled all of Europe and much of Russia. There was nowhere to go and not get caught and killed. Sweden and Switzerland were the only safe havens. Every path to those countries was through German-occupied countries.

For those like me that fled, we had immense guilt for leaving the people dearest to us behind. We did not know where we were going, what we would face, and where we would get food, water, shelter, weapons, and ammunition.

It was not an act of bravery; it was an act of stubbornness and determination. We would not let the Germans dictate when, where, and how we died. We were driven by seeking revenge for the blood of our families and the Jewish people before we, too, would be killed. Perhaps some would escape to tell the firsthand story of what happened to the Jews of Europe.

So, when asking this question, why did the Jews allow themselves to be led to slaughter without resistance? Imagine being a broken person physically and mentally, having all sense of self-respect and self-esteem destroyed. You are starving, sick, cold, wet, beaten and tortured mentally and physically daily. And you have no weapons or means to fight back. And any act of defiance, or even a perceived act of defiance, resulted in the immediate death of other family members and community members by the Germans in retribution. How can anyone under these conditions offer outright resistance?

And so, people walked and boarded the transport trains silent and passively as all the pictures show. They were silent and passive as they stood in front of firing squads. They were silent and passive as they entered the gas chambers. There was no other way or choice for them. Death was the only path to freedom for them.

For those like me who fled, the following questions help explain the feelings and emotions we had to deal with:

1. *Who can understand a person's feelings when he is forced to leave all his property and belongings that he worked for all his life and flee? When there is nowhere to go because he is marked wherever he goes. And everyone, including his Gentile neighbors, is watching and waiting to loot his home and possessions.*

2. *And who can understand a person's feelings when he comes to the very end of the road and is caged in a ghetto and treated far worse than an animal?*

3. *And who can understand a person's feelings when faced with death and must choose between running away and leaving all his dearest family with the murderers or staying with them to the very end? Or to run away into the unknown, knowing he is marked, has a price on his head, and can trust no one?*

4. *And who can understand the feelings of a person when his family tells him there is no place to go and you will only delay the inevitable. That there is no escaping the Germans, no matter where you go!*

5. *And who can understand a person's feelings when he must tell his dearest family that he must flee and die on his terms? And then say goodbye, knowing they were to be transported to the death camps within days.*

6. *And who can advise which is better, active or passive resistance? My brother and I fled and survived the partisan life. It can only be for the memory of all who died and to show the world that the Jewish people cannot be destroyed.*

Many people believed back then leaving your family to flee into the forest was considered being a coward. There is a valid argument that the actual heroes are our dearest family members that we left behind and perished through their acts of passive resistance to the end. Imagine what they went through mentally and physically while on the trains and in the camps. That was bravery!

I know I would never have been able to deal with the indignities associated with being in a death camp. I was not brave enough to handle going to a death camp. Fleeing to the forest and fighting for revenge was a much easier path for me.

EPILOGUE

Life goes by so fast, with both the good and the bad. The bad helps us appreciate the good, even if that time is short. I cherish those last two weeks spent with my mother. It was a gift to both of us. I also realized my mother was right about something else. The Holocaust denied her the life she should have lived, but not in the way I initially thought she was saying. She should have been able to live her life without severe depression. She at least got a few months of that.

I also learned that not sharing who we are and where we came from, no matter how horrible that might be, is far worse than the upsets associated with sharing it. My parents and all Holocaust survivors had good intentions in shielding us from those atrocities. Still, there was far more damage by not sharing it. We already suffered from the pain and guilt without knowing why. Knowing their stories would have made us closer, happier, and supportive of one another. Our relationships would have been stronger and more fulfilled. My parents, especially my mother, would have gotten her needed help early on. She would have lived the life she should have lived.

All of us in the next generation and beyond live with big voids in our lives. Most grew up with no grandparents, no aunts or uncles. We have no roots. No past. We carry emotional scars. But we cannot be silent like our parents. We must tell our parents' stories, and we must tell our own. Telling these stories helps us heal. Telling these stories through every generation keeps them alive.

In writing this book, I have captured most of my parents' unknown stories, along with the essence of their pain and emotions. The demons in my head are not demons anymore. I took on a project for the first time, where I set out to prove something to myself, not to others. I know my parents would be happy and grateful that I pursued this endeavor.

My grandfather, Zeev Gritczak, proved that personal connections and relationships could eliminate barriers of ignorance and hate. While the Polish Christians were very antisemitic, he developed friendships through direct relationships. He and they were human beings to each other. Those relationships saved his family's lives.

It is human nature to be influenced by stereotypes, the herd mentality of fear and hate. Personal relationships with people who are different change that. If there were a way for all people to meet and know each other, perhaps the hatred of all people who are different would go away. Unfortunately, achieving this is an unrealistic expectation, which is tragically sad.

My father told me a long time ago that extremists and hate have always existed and will always exist. Both have existed for all of humankind. There is nothing magic that will make them go away. We think extremism and hate go away when they go undercover. I thought our country had made tremendous progress since the 1960s. New laws and our culture forced the extremists and haters to go underground. They have come back out because they have gained legitimacy and power. We thought the world learned from World War II. Putin and Russia have now uprooted world stability with the invasion of Ukraine.

Extremism and hate go undercover because they know they cannot get away with it. Extremists and haters must fear the consequences of their hate being known. That is the best we can do to control it.

If we allow the haters to gain power, they commit the atrocities known throughout history. The Holocaust is only one of those atrocities. There have been many holocausts since the Holocaust. The war in Ukraine is today's Holocaust.

The best we can do is to educate and connect with the ignorant. We must recognize that those who will not listen will never change. Those who believe lies and refuse to hear the truth will never change. The focus must be on keeping power away from the extremists and haters and forcing them underground. Let them live in fear, not us. We will not hurt or kill them. We must create consequences for their hate that shame and isolate them.

The Germans believed they were brave and invincible when they fought people who could not fight back. They flaunted their brutality on defenseless people. But when others fought back, they revealed the reality that they were cowards. They ran and crumbled. That is how haters with power have behaved throughout history. That is why they never prevailed. The human desire to be safe and free is stronger than any oppressor. The ingenuity and cleverness of the oppressed are more potent than any army.

When the Jews organized as partisans, the Germans feared every Jew behind the trees in the forests. They even feared the trees, not knowing if partisans were hiding behind them! The Warsaw ghetto uprising demonstrated how seven hundred fighters could push back an entire army for one month. Today, we do not need to run into the woods. We need to get off the sidelines and make a stand. Silence gives the haters their power.

The aftermath of the silence of the 1930s resulted in the deliberate extermination of 90 percent (six million) of European Jews and twenty million Russians killed. World War II resulted in seventy-five to eighty million lives lost. Most of Europe lay destroyed. Time after time, history confirms that nothing good ever comes out of right-wing nationalism and fascism, only the death and destruction of all involved. While the world paid a high price for Hitler's rise to power, Germany too was destroyed—all for one man's ego and hatred.

Today, the world faces the same threats my parents and their generation faced in the 1930s. America has always been a nation of finding common ground, of learning from our mistakes. America has never been perfect, but we have always strived to be better.

Today, I fear America's future. Extremists are exploiting our divisions. Social media and cable news are fueling the fire. Many political leaders are focused on allegiances to other people and not the country. Both political parties demonize each other. Civil disagreement and debate are a thing of the past.

January 6, 2021, was a shot across the bow of our democracy. We are deeply divided on whether January 6, 2021, was an insurrection intended to overthrow our government or an act of patriotism as people on the extreme claim.

January 6, 2021, is the same scenario as Hitler's Beer Hall Putsch in 1923, a failed coup. Hilter and his extremist followers claimed it was an act of patriotism.

After Hitler's coup failed, he became determined to take over the government by changing laws and taking people's rights away through false claims. He succeeded. The "big lie" about the 2020 election has extremist politicians and state legislatures doing the same in many states today.

As a Jew, the extremists with their hate and vitriol terrify me. Jews are one of their targets. So are other minority groups.

In Europe today, we see the most significant, most destructive war since World War II. Putin invaded Ukraine for the same reasons Hitler invaded and annexed Austria, then the Czech Republic, then Poland, then all of Europe and Russia. Putin's stated objective is to conquer Ukraine, and his actions are destroying Ukraine. Many innocent lives are being lost. Why? Because he wants to recreate the old Russian Empire. It is all about his ego, his power.

The world has responded to the war in Ukraine differently than the appeasement given to Hitler. But it is a war Ukraine has to fight alone for now. Would Putin be a madman and use nuclear weapons if other countries sent troops to Ukraine? Or would that action force Putin to back down? Reading the mind of a madman is impossible today, no different from in the 1930s. But somehow, Russia must be defeated.

Has the world learned from the past? I think not. Is the world on the path to even more war and destruction? Will democracy survive in America? I am worried. I am scared. Not so much for myself, but for the next generation and beyond. What will their lives be like in the years ahead?

I am glad my parents and most other survivors did not live long enough to see American democracy in crisis and the Russian invasion of Ukraine.

I hope that people worldwide wake up, see the destructive path we are on, and end it. We know the consequences if we don't.

One of my favorite songs has always been Simon and Garfunkel's "The Sound of Silence." Some have said Paul Simon wrote the song to express his concern about people's silent, blind allegiance to their leaders. The song is more relevant today than in the 1960s when it was written.

Like "The Sound of Silence," Ecclesiastes 3:1-8 has always had a special place in my heart. It goes back to The Byrds, who made it into a great song, but I always paid special attention when it was read in the synagogue. It always strikes a particular chord in me.

I often think about the verses when I reflect on the world and my own life. The challenges I face and the choices I make. There have been times of good and times of evil. What choices have I made? Did I stand up for what is right? What is the right thing to do now? How do we make the world a better place? My parents instilled this in my DNA. Their most precious gift to me was to teach me to care and make a difference.

Think about these words and the choices you make! Choose to do what is right. As America is divided and faces its very existence as a democracy, choose a time to love and not a time to hate! As the war and devastation continue in Ukraine, choose a time for peace and not a time for war!

> *For everything there is a season,*
> *A right time for every intention under heaven —*
> *A time to be born and a time to die,*
> *A time to plant and a time to uproot,*
> *A time to kill and a time to heal,*
> *A time to tear down and a time to build,*
> *A time to weep and a time to laugh,*
> *A time to mourn and a time to dance,*
> *A time to throw stones and a time to gather*
>   *stones,*
> *A time to embrace and a time to refrain,*
> *A time to search and a time to give up,*
> *A time to keep and a time to discard,*
> *A time to tear and a time to sew,*
> *A time to keep silent and a time to speak,*
> *A time to love and a time to hate,*
> *A time for war and a time for peace.*

Left to right, Sandi, Jerry, Janet, David, Emily (David's wife), October 2019

APPENDIXES

APPENDIXES

APPENDIX

DRAFT OUTLINE OF MEMOIRS WRITTEN IN YIDDISH AND RECENTLY TRANSLATED

I n 1975 my brother, Ben, and I tried to convince our father to translate his Yiddish published diary and write his memoirs. He started to write some things in Yiddish and quickly stopped, saying he did not want to write his story.

1) *Prużana [now Pruzhany, Belarus], Poland (youth – education – dreams – beginning of the war – life in ghetto – burgermeister .and liquidation – breakthrough and group tensions).*

2) *Trukhonovichi, Zamosze [now Zamošša, Belarus], [Zaveski? – unidentified place name] forest, Janin, Różana [now Ruzhany, Belasrus] forest, Kirov, detachment, Mikhalin, Kalinin detachment; battles in Nowy Dwór, Białowieża Forest, defeat – [Khoroshch?/Kharashch? – unidentified place name] and the surrounding area, return to Białowieża, march back to Pinsk marshes, [Lipetzianker? – unidentified place name] woods, Moskali – Krupitzy and battles in the triangle between the Shchara [river] and the Neman [river] – Slonim – Jawor forest – Zdzięcioł [now Dzyatlava, Belarus] – Wołkowysk [now Vawkavysk, Belarus] – Zelwa [now Zelva, Belarus].*

3) Liberation and new problems. Wołkowysk, Grodno. Back in Prużana, Białowieża, Bielsk - Brańsk — frontline — back in Wołkowysk.

4) Bialystok — Warsaw — Lodz — Cracow — Bratislava — Vienna — the Alps — Tyrol mountains — Trofaiach — Graz — Williach — Salzburg — Munich — Germany — Feldafing — Neu Freimann — Bremen and Syracuse. First work. Business.

2

APPENDIX

IMMIGRATION CORRESPONDENCE
LETTERS

A PPENDIX 2
The effort to get visas for the Elman family for entry into the United States is a story in and of itself. Without the relentless work of Samuel and IJ Elman, Louis's uncle and cousin, my parents and brother would have never made it to the United States. They first faced the bureaucracy of all the agencies involved. Then, the criminal record for Louis having sixty American dollars, not knowing it was illegal, became an almost insurmountable barrier. The American Consul General approved Germans and Poles who had killed Jews but refused to approve Shmeryl because of this minor crime. The Consul General would not reverse his decision throughout this effort, no matter the pressure. So, they changed their names and applied with those new names. The Consul General then quickly approved the visa for Leib Wacht, not knowing it was Shmeryl Elman.

The following is a sample of the volumes of correspondence pursued by Samuel and IJ Elman. My parents were always grateful to both. Samuel passed away in 1971; IJ in 1983.

The original copies of the letters kept by Samuel and IJ were typed using carbon paper and photocopied many years later.

These were illegible for book publishing. Therefore, those letters have been retyped word for word for use in this book.

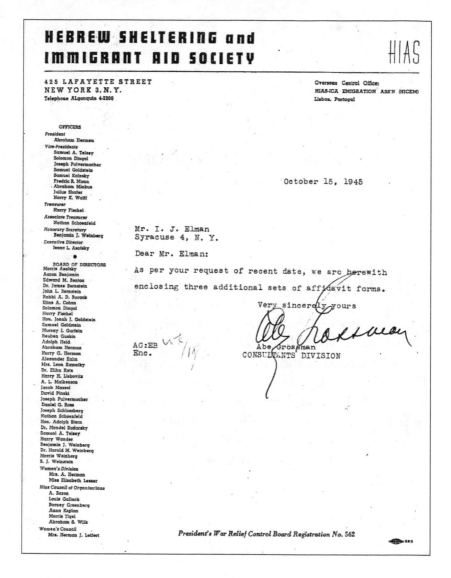

HEBREW SHELTERING and IMMIGRANT AID SOCIETY

HIAS

425 LAFAYETTE STREET
NEW YORK 3, N.Y.
Telephone ALgonquin 4-2900

Overseas Central Office:
HIAS-ICA EMIGRATION ASS'N (HICEM)
Lisbon, Portugal

December 11, 1945

Mr. Samuel Elman
1050 West Genesee St.
Syracuse, N.Y.

RE: Szmerko ELMAN
Josel   "
_ _ _Poland_ _ _ _ _

Dear Mr. Elman:

We are in receipt of yours of November 21st in the matter of the above-named, and after reviewing the documents, we suggest you comply with the instructions clearly outlined to you in the enclosed memorandum.

We are returning the statements with the following comments:

1. Your employer's statement is not notarized.
2. Two copies of the income tax return are needed.
3. Your bank letters indicating personal savings are lacking.

4. Original bond statement is lacking and these of course also have to be notarized. *(seal)*

5. Affidavits themselves are not notarized and we note we only have the carbon copies.

After completion, all copies duly notarized, kindly forward the original and duplicate together with the supporting financial statements, in duplicate, directly to your relative abroad for presentation to the American Consul.

In addition, send us two copies of the affidavit, so that we may communicate with our European office for purposes of assisting in obtaining a visa for your relatives, and also arrange transportation just as soon as it becomes available.

Very sincerely yours,

Abe Grossman
CONSULTANTS DIVISION

AG:hs
Enc.

President's War Relief Control Board Registration No. 562

May 29, 1946

Hebrew Sheltering & Immigrant Aid Society
425 Lafayette Street
New York 3, New York

Attn.: Mr. William Males

Dear Mr. Wales:

In accordance with your letter of May 16th, we are enclosing herewith:

1. Affidavits of Mr. Samuel Elman original and duplicate covering Szmerko Elman and Josel Elman.
2. Original and Duplicate affidavit of Samuel Elman Co. employer of Samuel Elman certifying his income.
3. Original and duplicate of affidavit of Thomas W. Higgins, Vice President of the Merchants National Bank and Trust Co., of Syracuse New York, verifying the assets and income of Samuel Elman.
4. Original and photostat of list of bonds owned by Mr. Samuel Elman (you will note that the photostat could not take the date nor would the notarized seal come through on it).
5. Original and photostat of personal financial statement of Mr. Samuel Elman (the notarial seal did not transfer to the photostat, but it appears on the original).
6. Original and photostat of income tax return for 1945 of Mr. Samuel Elman.

These are the documents specified to be submitted to you by your Mr. Grossman in a letter dated December 11th.
If you will note the location of the nephews is Camp Feldafing

near Munich in Germany and therefore according to your letter of May 16th, you handle it through your office.

We will greatly appreciate your expediting any action on this and if there is any expense involved that should be charged to us Mr. Samuel Elman, please do not hesitate to write us.

Very truly yours,
  IJ Elman

IJE:TS
Enc.-6

P.S.—The address we now have was given to us May 6th, 1946, and we assume that they are still there.

May 31, 1946

Mr. William Rosenwald
National Refugee Service
105 Nassau Street
New York 7, New York

My dear Mr. Rosenwald:

Your files will reveal that on February 1st Mr. Samuel M. Schmidt of Cincinnati, Ohio, who is my mother's brother, wrote you with reference to two of my cousins on my father's side, who are now in the American-occupied zone of Germany.

On May 29th, all necessary papers were forwarded to the Hebrew Sheltering and Immigrant Aid Society to the attention of Mr. William Males. The address of these refugees is as follows:

Szmerko and Josel Elman

Munich 13 C—
Nei Freiman Sidlung,
Gundelkofer Str. 8
U.S.A Zone
Deutschland, Bavaria

Any additional cooperation you can give will be more than appreciated for it is a favor to us and to Mr. Schmidt.

Please note that the contribution to the United Jewish Appeal on the part of my father and myself as well on the part of the Jewish employees of this Company as well as the writer's personal efforts in the campaign have been highly commended on by the leaders of the campaign as being liberal and wholehearted.

Very truly yours,
IJ Elman

IJE:TS

May 31, 1946

Mr. Moses Leavitt, Secretary
Joint Distribution Committee
270 Madison Avenue
New York, New York

My dear Mr. Leavitt:

Your files will reveal that on February 1st Mr. Samuel M. Schmidt of Cincinnati, Ohio, who is my mother's brother, wrote you with reference to two of my cousins on my father's side, who are now in the American-occupied zone of Germany.

On May 29th, all necessary papers were forwarded to the Hebrew Sheltering and Immigrant Aid Society to the attention of Mr. William Males. The address of these refugees is as follows:

Szmerko and Josel Elman
Munich 13 C—
Nei Freiman Sidlung,
Gundelkofer Str. 8
U.S.A Zone
Deutschland, Bavaria

Any additional cooperation you can give will be more than appreciated for it is a favor to us and to Mr. Schmidt.

Please note that the contribution to the United Jewish Appeal on the part of my father and myself as well on the part of the Jewish employees of this Company as well as the writer's personal efforts in the campaign have been highly commended on by the leaders of the campaign as being liberal and wholehearted.

Very truly yours,
    IJ Elman

IJE:TS

811.11 ELMAN, Szmerko, Josel
TAM:mg   and Rochel

THE FOREIGN SERVICE
OF THE
UNITED STATES OF AMERICA

American Consulate General,
Munich, Germany, October 3, 1946.

The Honorable
    Clarence E. Hancock,
        House of Representatives,
            Washington, D. C.

Sir:

The Consulate General has received your letter of
August 29, 1946 relative to your interest in the immigration
to the United States of Szmerko, Josel and Rochel ELMAN.

The files of the Consulate General include a personal
data sheet filed by Szmerko, Josel and Rochel Elman through
the United Nations Relief and Rehabilitation Administration
for preliminary examination. The information given on the
sheet indicates that the applicants are chargeable to the
Polish quota. As this office has far more applicants who
fall under that quota than it has Polish quota numbers
available, it is not possible to estimate when a quota number
will become available for Szmerko, Josel and Rochel Elman's
use and when they will be invited to call at the Consulate
General to file a formal application for their immigration
visa.

You may be sure, however, that at such time as a quota
number becomes available for Szmerko, Josel and Rochel Elman's
use and they make their formal application, their case will be
given careful consideration.

Very truly yours,

James R. Wilkinson,
American Consul General.

HEBREW SHELTERING and IMMIGRANT AID SOCIETY

HIAS

425 LAFAYETTE STREET
NEW YORK 3, N.Y.
Telephone ORchard 4-6900

Overseas Central Office:
Paris, France

October 30, 1946

Mr. I. J. Elman
Samuel Elman Co., Inc.
Syracuse 4, New York

Re: Elman, Szmerko, Josel
Deutchland, Bavaria.

Dear Mr. Elman:

This will acknowledge receipt of your communication of October 11th, 1946.

Since the immigrants have acquired a newly born son, it will be necessary that you execute an affidavit in behalf of the new born child.

For this purpose, we are enclosing two copies of affidavits which you should fill in and mail back to our office. We will then forward these copies to our representative in Germany.

Very sincerely yours,

D. Gralen
CONSULTANTS DIVISION

DG:RS
ENCL.

JERRY M. ELMAN

March 28, 1947

Mr. I.J. Elman   Re: ELMAN, Szmerko & Josel
Samuel Elman Co. Inc.   Munich 13 C
Syracuse 4, N.Y.   Nei Freiman Sidlung
                                        Gundelkofer Str. 8
                                        U.S. zone, Germany
My dear Mr. Elman: Our Case #1033

    Your communication has just reached my desk since I
have been previously handling the correspondence regarding your
relatives.

    Please be assured that we fully sympathize with your
concern at the delay of your relative's immigration. In order
to obtain a report on their present status we have communicated
once more with our overseas office. We will be glad to pass their
reply along to you.

    At the same time may we again point out to you that the
report from overseas, which we received previously and passed on
to you on August 13th, definitely stated that the case of your
relatives is being handled by HIAS and not by our organization.
It might be wise, therefore, for you to also follow this matter
up with the HIAS.

Sincerely yours,

Personal Service Department
Reta L. Stein, Director

ece/sk

206

March 26, 1947

Mr. Moses Leavitt, Secretary
Joint Distribution Committee
270 Madison Ave.
New York, New York

Re: Szmerko and Josel Elman
    Munich 13C
    Nei Freiman Sidling
    Gundelkofer Str. 8
    USA Zone
    Deutschland, Bavaria

Dear Mr. Leavitt:

Just to refresh your memory, I am the nephew of Mr. Samuel
M. Schmidt of Cincinnati, Ohio and I am again writing to you on
behalf of my two cousins who are languishing in the above camp.

Whether there is any connection or not, I must point out that
last year we contributed very liberally to the annual United Jewish
Appeal and we intend to be a liberal as possible this year. Isn't
there any possible way of <u>doing something</u> for these poor
refugees? There must be some points that can be stretched in view
of all the circumstances involved.

Are there any angles or roundabout methods of
accomplishing the result of bringing them here? It will be two
years that we have been trying to do this and I earnestly request
that you give this your personal attention toward this end.

Sincerely yours,

IJ Elman

IJE:TS

April 3, 1947

Hon. James R. German
United States Consul General
Munich, Germany

Re: Szmerko and Josel Elman
      Munich 13C—
      Nei Freiman Sidling
      Gundelkofer Str. 3, U.S.A Zone
      Deutschland, Bavaria

Honorable Sir:

   Your files will indicate a letter written to you by our mutual friend, Clarence E. Hancock, then US congressman from our locality, also a letter I wrote to you on October 4th, 1946, regarding the above refugees. We have just been advised that one of them, Josel Elman has been summoned for his visa but that Szmerko, his wife Rachel, and their child are being held up because of some cloud over the record of Szmerko. As we are informed, when he went from Austria to Munich, he was found with some American money in his possession which is apparently an infraction of the law.

   It would be improper on my part to in any way insinuate that a violator of the law should not be punished for that particular violation. The only point I want to make is that these poor devils have been punished beyond all reason for no crime at all and where it is generally agreed that the "punishment must fit the crime," here is a case where no crime on earth could have been great enough to "fit" the punishment they have endured in the war.

We hear constant reports, whether true or not, of individuals and groups being pardoned, and even go scot-free after committing terrible crimes under the Nazi Regime. This in itself is no justification for asking any particular favor for Szmerko Elman, or his wife and child.

The cloud or black mark against his conduct, while apparently real, cannot possibly be enough to offset the terrible ordeals that they have endured <u>plus</u> the fact that Szmerko Elman during his years with the guerrillas, actually killed numerous of our enemy.

The burden of maintaining these unfortunates in your DP camps is a great one and we here in America are ready and willing to relieve that burden to the extent of our own dependents. We are ready, willing and anxious to assume complete responsibility for their shelter, maintenance and usefulness to society.

Is there any court higher than the court of humanity, and if said, Szmerko Elman, committed the crime charged against him, I am sure that not only was it done without malice or fraud or <u>intent</u> to violate any laws not only that but perhaps it was done during a period of utter terror, fear or hysteria after the years of grueling animal like existence that he endured after seeing his parents and sisters murdered before his eyes not only that but even if there were no extenuating elements, still the punishment has already far exceeded this particular crime as well as the total absence of guilt on his part or on the part of any of the other millions of Jews who underwent the Nazi tortures.

Fortunately, the visa for his brother, Josel, is apparently now being granted. Is there any other thing that you can do to personally look into this particular case and see what can be done?

. . .

Very truly yours,
  IJ Elman

IJE:TS

_____

April 11, 1947

Hebrew Sheltering & Immigrant Aid Society
425 Lafayette Street
New York 5, New York

Re: Szmerko and Josel Elman
   Munich 13C—
   Nei Freiman Sidling
   Gundelkofer Str. 3, U.S.A Zone
   Deutschland, Bavaria

Gentlemen:

   We have received a letter from the above-mentioned refugees advising us that one of them, Josel Elman, has been called up for his visa but that Szmerko is being held up.

   The reason is that on Szmerko's entry into Munich from Austria he was found with some American money on his person. At that time, he was incarcerated for one month and it appears now that his record contains that particular infraction which is holding up his visa.

   No one knows better than your organization the terrific sufferings that these people have undergone and it would seem that perhaps something could be done so that he is not permitted to suffer any longer even though he undoubtfully did violate one of the rules and regulations.

   Is it possible for you to give this some extra personal attention to see what, if anything, can be done? We wish to remind you that Szmerko now has a wife named Rachel and an infant son.

Very truly yours,
    IJ Elman

IJ:TS

———————

May 1, 1947

Major Abraham Hyman
Office of Rabbi P.S. Bernstein
Adviser of Jewish Affairs to the Commander in Chief
Headquarters Eucom, APC 757, New York

AIR MAIL

Re: Szmerko and Rachel Elman & infant son
    Munich 13C—
    Nei Freiman Sidling
    Gundelkofer Str. 3, U.S.A Zone
    Deutschland, Bavaria

Dear Major Hyman:

The writer has just finished talking long distance to Rabbi Bernstein who has been a close personal friend since early college days at Syracuse University and after outlining to him the facts and circumstances of the problem confronting us, he suggested that I write to you with as full force as if he were writing these facts to you.

My two cousins escaped from the Nazis in Poland and for a number of years were associated with the guerrillas. The rest of their family, consisting of parents and several sisters, were murdered. The two boys drifted to Austria and finally ended up in the above camp. About a year ago we forwarded the necessary affidavits and guarantees to the Consul at Munich and early in April 1947 we received word that Josel Elman, the younger brother, had been called up for a visa. The older brother, Szmerko, the subject of our present communication, was bypassed because of an infraction of the regulations and as he tells us he was found with $60.00 of American money which he carried from Poland through Austria and into Munich. He has repeatedly stated that he brought this money from Poland and was unaware that he was violating any laws in having money in his possession.

These facts were embodied in a strong appeal to Consul Wilkinson at Munich, but Szmerko continued to be bypassed.

Now we are informed that his wife and infant son were called before the consul on April 15th and here begins the tragic part of this problem as Szmerko has delayed for one month the actual visa for his wife and son in not knowing whether he should permit his family to be disrupted and separated in permitting them to go to America and then take the chance on coming at a later date.

The approach to this problem is whether Szmerko's infraction was so great as to prevent him from getting his visa now or in the near future and then trying to decide whether he shall let his wife and son get their visas and not be separated from him until some indefinite time in the future.

As Szmerko puts it in his letter dated April 19th, "I have no one here who is able to intervene for me, and those under whose jurisdiction this under are not interested."

After languishing all three years waiting for a visa, it seems somewhat tragic to have it withheld for a minor infraction.

Both Rabbi Bernstein and I will deem it a great favor if you inject yourself into this matter personally, study the case, if possible, interview the principals and satisfy yourself as to what degree of seriousness his crime was and then use your best judgment as to what to do.

We want to remove these people from Europe thereby easing the burden of the Army and the authorities in caring for them.

I can think of nothing more to say except but to appeal to you to exert every possible effort and leave no stone unturned to bring this matter to its best conclusion and I have the assurance of Rabbi Bernstein that you will do so.

Sincerely yours,
IJ Elman

IJE:TS

P.S.—The time is short, exceedingly short, as Szmerko must decide between now and May 15th whether to let his family's visas lapse or take it up and have them separated from him. In other words, quick action is of the utmost importance so as to have it decided before May 15th.

cc: Rabbi P.S. Bernstein

———

May 5, 1947

Mr. Siegmund Lifschitz
Consultants Division
Hebrew Sheltering and Immigrant Aid Society
425 Lafayette St.
New York 3, New York

Re: Szmerko Elman
     Bavaria, Germany

. . .

Dear Mr. Lifschitz:

In your letter of May 2nd, you state that you cannot find any record of having placed a request for an additional deposit. I am enclosing herewith your mimeographed letter dated April 21st signed by yourself, to clear your records.

Now I have another urgent matter that has to be decided quickly. We have received word that Josel Elman has already been called for his visa as you no doubt know. At the same time, Szmerko was refused a visa because of an infraction that he committed a couple of years ago when he entered Munich from Austria, sixty dollars of American money having been found on his person. We immediately wrote a letter to Consul Wilkinson trying to get this infraction set aside.

We have now been informed that his wife Rachel and infant son were called for their visas on April 15th but that he is still being refused his visa because of the same infraction. The wife and child requested a thirty-day delay before deciding what to do, whether to accept their visas and come over here without her husband, Szmerko, or refuse their visas and take their chances on Szmerko being called up in a short time.

The time limit expires May 15th just ten days from today, after which we understand the wife and child will then go back to the bottom of the list and have to wait maybe years to come up again. We must ask that you cable your representative and ascertain which of the above alternatives he should accept.

If there will be only a short period of delay between the wife and child receiving their visas and coming to America and then subsequent granting of a visa to the husband Szmerko, that is one decision to make, but if there will be a prolonged delay and separation then that would be another decision to make. In no event, does it seem reasonable for this family to be torn apart again.

We will reimburse you for any cable costs that you incur and must ask that you give this your immediate attention.

. . .

Very truly yours,
    IJ Elman

IJ:TS
Enc.

———

May 8, 1947

Mr. I. J. Elman
c/o Samuel Elman Co., Inc.,
Syracuse 4, N.Y.

Re: ELMAN, Szmerko & Josel
Munich 13 C
Nei Freiman Sidlung
Gundelkofer Str. 8
U.S. Zone, Germany
Our Case #1033

My dear Mr. Elman:

We have just been advised by our overseas office that they are contacting
the U.S. Consulate in order to ascertain the emigration status of the
above named.

You may be certain that as soon as we have further news, we will be glad
to forward same to you.

Sincerely yours,

Personal Service Dept.,
Reta L. Stein, Director

ECE:ME

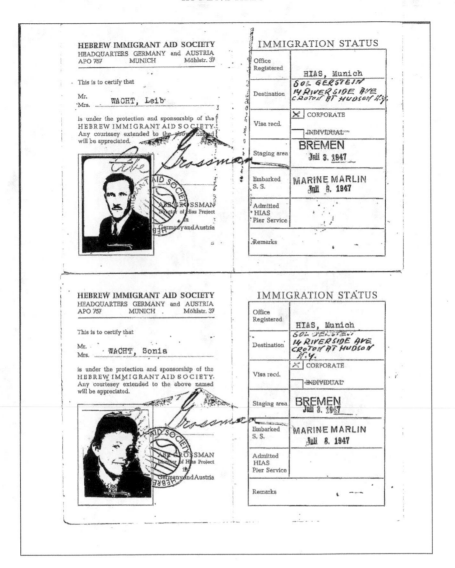

HEBREW IMMIGRANT AID SOCIETY
HEADQUARTERS GERMANY and AUSTRIA
APO 757   MUNICH   Möhlstr. 37

This is to certify that

Mr.
Mrs.   WACHT, Leib

is under the protection and sponsorship of the
HEBREW IMMIGRANT AID SOCIETY.
Any courtesey extended to the above named
will be appreciated.

ABE GROSSMAN
Director of Hias Project
in
Germany and Austria

IMMIGRATION STATUS	
Office Registered	HIAS, Munich
Destination	SOL GERSTEIN 14 RIVERSIDE AVE CROTON AT HUDSON N.Y.
Visa recd.	☒ CORPORATE / INDIVIDUAL
Staging area	**BREMEN** Juli 3. 1947
Embarked S. S.	**MARINE MARLIN** Juli 8. 1947
Admitted HIAS Pier Service	
Remarks	

HEBREW IMMIGRANT AID SOCIETY
HEADQUARTERS GERMANY and AUSTRIA
APO 757   MUNICH .   Möhlstr. 37

This is to certify that

Mr.
Mrs.   WACHT, Sonia

is under the protection and sponsorship of the
HEBREW IMMIGRANT AID SOCIETY.
Any courtesey extended to the above named
will be appreciated.

ABE GROSSMAN
Director of Hias Project
in
Germany and Austria

IMMIGRATION STATUS	
Office Registered	HIAS, Munich
Destination	SOL GERSTEIN 14 RIVERSIDE AVE CROTON AT HUDSON N.Y.
Visa recd.	☒ CORPORATE / INDIVIDUAL
Staging area	**BREMEN** Juli 3. 1947
Embarked S. S.	**MARINE MARLIN** Juli 8. 1947
Admitted HIAS Pier Service	
Remarks	

3

APPENDIX

OBITUARY OF SAMUEL ELMAN

Samuel Elman, Louis and Joseph's uncle, was a remarkable person beyond his effort to bring them to America. He was a man of strong beliefs who not only cared about his family, but he also cared for his employees and his community. Samuel passed away on June 8, 1971, at the age of 101. The following is his obituary:

Samuel Elman was born in a little village named Lisniki (Russia) in 1870. As a young man seeing no future for him in Russia, he took off for the New World. In 1891 after many months of travel, he arrived in New York City to start a new life.

While working a few years in a clothing factory, he was active in organizing the first union movement in the New York City garment industry and later became a business agent for the union.

In 1894, in a time of crisis in the vest coat industry, he organized a cooperative vest shop in Boston and married there. In 1898 he moved to Syracuse, NY, became a vest contractor, gave it up, and later opened up his own pants factory.

In the beginning, he employed eighteen operators and gradually increased his operations and grew larger. As he succeeded in business, he always increased the benefits for his employees. As early as 1918, he provided free dental care for all his employees and built individual chairs for his operators to suit everyone's height in order to make their workday easier. Over a period of fifty years his business became nationally known.

He never forgot his large family which he left behind in Russia. One by one he brought four of his sisters and their families to the United States, where they built a new life for themselves. After World War II he brought over the last two survivors of his family from the Hitler Holocaust.

In 1930, Samuel Elman was critically injured in an automobile accident, after which he lost one arm. He spent many months in the hospital, fought back to recover and took his disability in stride. He became active again in his company. But in 1956 tragedy struck again as his famous son, Dr. Robert Elman, of St. Louis, died of a heart attack at the age of fifty-nine. Dr. Elman made great contributions in medicine, specializing in the treatment of malaria during World War II in the Pacific area of the war. He also developed innovative approaches in surgery and recovery and was nationally recognized for his work.

A second son, Leon Elman, died in Miami, Florida, and once again that was a severe blow to him. Hurt spiritually, Samuel Elman retired and moved to Miami, Florida. His third son, Isadore (IJ) Elman ran the business until a few years later it was decided to offer the business to the employees as a form of a cooperative. When this offer did not materialize, the Samuel Elman Manufacturing Company, in business for over fifty years, closed its doors. Out of the income from the business liquidation, Samuel Elman donated $70,000 to the Jewish Home for the Aged of Central New York.

In Miami, Mr. Elman was also active and contributed greatly to charitable organizations. He contributed to several projects in Israel, one was to build a trade school for young boys, in the name of his son Dr. Robert Elman. He was also one of the first subscribers to the Jewish Daily Forward since the very first issue. Samuel Elman was also a member of the Golden Ring Club Number One, of the Workman's Circle of America.

During all those years in America, Samuel Elman only went overseas once. That was for the occasion of the birth of the State of Israel in 1950. He became an enthusiastic contributor to the Israel labor union called Histadrut. Upon his death, he donated a large part of his estate to Israel.

Despite his old age, he was very alert and had a strong memory up to his death. He was interested in world and local affairs, read many newspapers and took long daily walks. He influenced the Jewish Daily Forward, which only published in Yiddish, to publish a special page in English in every Sunday edition. As the generation that read Yiddish declined, he saw an opportunity for the newspaper to connect with the next generation in English.

Written by his son, IJ Elman

4

APPENDIX

DAVID ELMAN'S FIFTH-GRADE WRITING PROJECT ABOUT HIS GRANDMOTHER, RACHEL ELMAN

This was handwritten in cursive. David's fifth-grade teacher was meticulous in teaching cursive.

My Grandma, Sonia Rachel Elman
by David Elman

On November 10, 1927, a very special person was brought to the world to add one more person to the Gitchock family, someone who was born in a quiet city called Sokoly, Poland. This is someone who lived with a great family, went to a good school for only twelve years, and had a lot of fun when she was my age. Can you guess who she is? She's my grandma! My grandma just became a septuagenarian on November 10th. She was born in Sokoly, Poland, and her first and last name in Poland was Rachel Gitchock. When she came to the United States in 1947, they named her Sonia Rachel Elman. Her last name changed in 1946 when she got married to my grandpa, Louis Elman.

My grandma lived in Sokoly, Poland, until she was twelve years old and then she was taken to a ghetto for two years under German occupation when World War 2 began in 1939. The ghettos were cities that were fenced up and guarded by the Germans. My grandma lived with her mother, father, and sister, but she only lived with her brother for twelve years because he was taken to a concentration camp by the Germans, where he died. My grandma lived in a pretty good city before she and her family were taken to a ghetto. The city was very quiet and peaceful. Every neighbor knew each other, and they helped each other when they needed help with a chore, etc. When my grandma and her family lived in the ghetto for two years, they were fenced up and they could only go to work and back. It was very hard living in the ghetto. You can see so far that my grandma's life was much different than mine is.

There was no Nintendo, no television, no computers, no stereo, and no tapes or CD's. Even though my grandma didn't have all of these Hi-tech objects that I do, it didn't stop her from having a lot of fun. My grandma did many activities when she had spare time. She did after school activities, liked playing volleyball and doing gymnastics. She loved to ice skate, she played table pool, and she had the best of times sledding in the snow. She was a really good cook, she listened to the radio, and like everybody, she loved to eat. My grandma didn't do very many chores at home. All my she had to do for chores was the tedious house cleaning. She liked cooking, and she went shopping for her mother.

My grandma's school wasn't much different than the schools now-a-days. My grandma loved school and she did very well in it. Her school was very challenging for her, and the teachers were very kind and helpful like they are now. The name of the school was just "Public School". The grades were kindergarten through 7th grade, and they met Monday through Thursday, from 8:00 A.M. to 3:00 P.M. The school was a pretty good size, and there were about 420 students. Now you can see why her school wasn't much different than Thornell Road School.

My grandma had a lot of momentous days in her life. Some were bad experiences and some were good experiences. The first memory she had was when the Germans made she and her family leave their home in the ghetto, and then the Germans burned the house and all of my grandma's possessions. My grandma and her family then had to move to a Polish farm with nothing. The next memory was a bad experience, too. She remembered when her brother was taken to a concentration camp by the Germans, where he was killed. The next two memories she had are happy moments in her life. The war ended and the Russians liberated the Jews and they were all freed. That was one of the happiest moments in her life. The last one she remembered was when she came to the United States in 1947. She's been in the United States for almost 51 years!

My grandma also had memories about her family. She remembers when her family was all split up after the war ended because some people died and a lot of her family was still alive, and when she started a whole new life in the United States with my grandpa, Louis Elman.

Sonia Rachel Elman is a very special person in my life because she is very kind, generous, and loving. Even though she had a lot of obstacles, she still a really fulfilled, joyous life and those obstacles didn't change her personality at all. My grandma is clearly the best grandma in the world! I hope you learned a lot about my incredible grandma and how she handled her obstacles in her life!

5

APPENDIX

MAPS

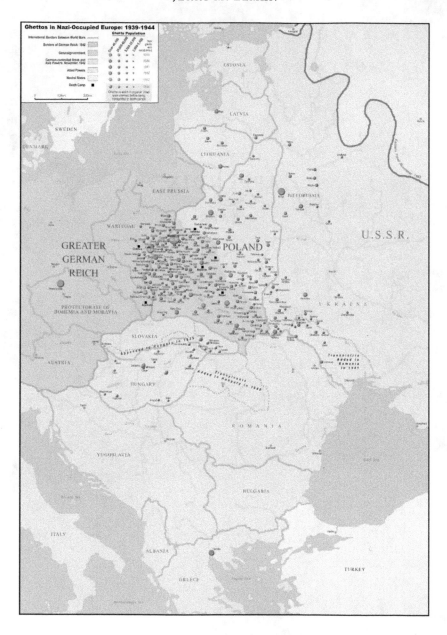

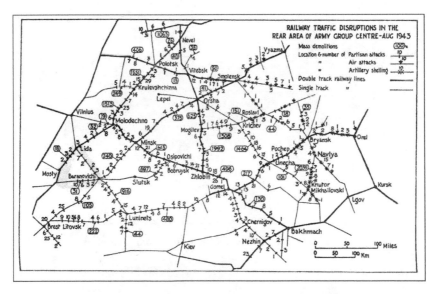

Triangle is area Shmeryl Elman's partisan unit controlled

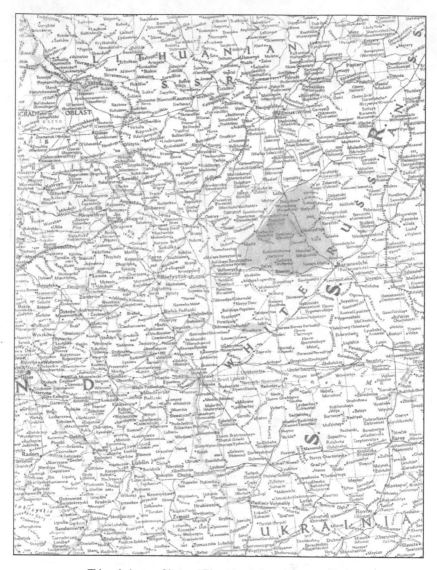

Triangle is area Shmeryl Elman's partisan unit controlled

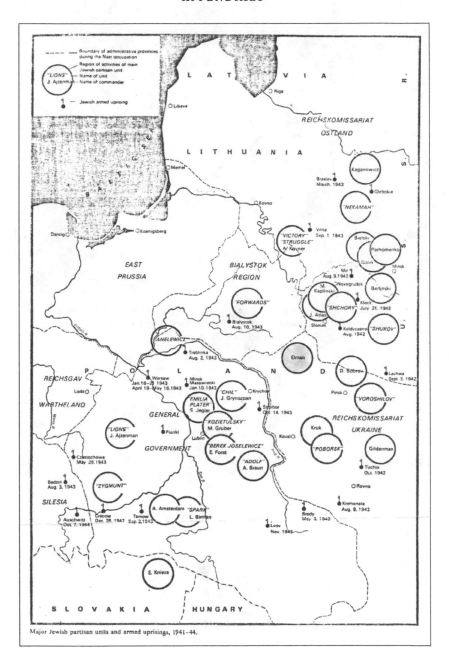

Major Jewish partisan units and armed uprisings, 1941-44.

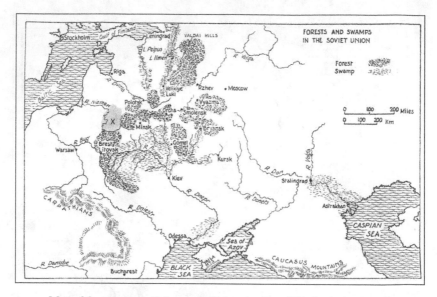

Map of forest areas in Belarus and Bialystok region. This forest density was
ideal for partisan groups to operate within. Shmeryl Elman's partisan unit
controlled the X area.

ABOUT THE AUTHOR

Jerry Elman was born in 1954 in Syracuse, NY. He has lived in the Rochester, NY area for almost fifty years. Jerry is a first-generation American whose parents were both Holocaust survivors. Jerry lived most of his life not knowing his parents' stories or his European roots and family. His father passed away in 1989, his mother in 2004.

Jerry retired in 2021 and the desire to know his parents' stories kept nagging at him. At age sixty-seven he began searching files and documents his parents left behind that had some information. He started his research effort and one piece of information led to another piece of information. Connecting with resources at the US Holocaust Museum, Yad Vashem in Israel, YIVO, JewishGen, the USC Shoah Project, and other resources, Jerry found all the information that became the basis for writing this book.

This is his first book written and published. It is a work of love and closure to questions never answered most of his life. Writing this book was a cathartic experience for Jerry.

CPSIA information can be obtained
at www.ICGtesting.com
Printed in the USA
BVHW030938220722
642540BV00007B/162/J